TABLE
FOR TWO

TABLE
FOR
TWO

Recipes for the
ones you love

Bre Graham

Part I

EASY TO IMPRESS

Part II

JUST TO DELIGHT

Table for Two

(recipes for the ones you love)

"It seems to me that our three basic needs, for food and security and love, are so mixed and mingled and entwined that we cannot straightly think of one without the others. So it happens that when I write of hunger, I am really writing about love and the hunger for it, and warmth and the love of it and the hunger for it ... There is communion of more than our bodies when bread is broken and wine drunk."

The Gastronomical Me, M.F.K. Fisher, 1943

Sharing food at a table set for two is where some of the most important moments of my life have taken place. There are times for tables of 10, solo self-love meals, and dinner parties that end on a dancefloor, but a table for two is something special. The intimacy and immediacy of sitting with someone and enjoying a meal made with love can make the noise of the outside world calm and quiet. These are the days when you open another bottle of wine while listening to stories about your mother's life before you were born; or when you handwrite a menu for an anniversary meal you couldn't have even imagined possible a few years ago.

I've spent the last 10 years thinking about little else than cooking and love. What I've learnt with each failed romance and every finished meal is that it's best to risk failure and delight in both. For a brief period in my twenties, the only things in my life that went to plan were recipes. I'm originally from Sydney but grew up in Singapore and moved to London at 18 so for much of my life

I've felt homesick for someone or somewhere. Among my feelings of loneliness, being far away from family, I got caught up in the ache of looking for love. There were crash and burn crushes, lots of those brief flirtations that floor you, with men that started as gods and ended up as ghosts. I'd stay up all night and bake birthday cakes for people I hardly knew and throw parties for friends of friends that I'd spend a week's wages on the ingredients for, and then the next two days cleaning up afterwards.

In between university lectures on literature (that I barely attended) I was a dog walker, a nanny, and an office assistant at the famed London restaurant, St. John, as well as spending every spare minute hungry for someone to call my own as I went home each night to cook alone. Until I really knew who I was, I looked for love in all the wrong people and places; I lost myself for a while among the longing, but those years taught me that love leaks into our lives in more ways than one - sometimes we just need to see it.

Opening my eyes to the romance of a night spent eating pizza on a park bench with my best friend; making a lamb stew for my Dad and I to share; or the awkward early days of getting to know someone new, all helped to lift a weight off my shoulders and let me feel the love that was already around me. I don't believe romance should be just reserved for romantic love. In my eyes, it is something we can imbue every occasion with, not only for a girlfriend/husband/partner; our lives are full of so many other people worthy of a little romance.

Define what brings you joy and make all occasions matter: recreate your brother's favourite restaurant menu; fill your friend's glass with the amaro you brought back from your last holiday together, because what we cook for people we love forms our shared stories. These meals bind our lives together and are what we pass down to those who in time will watch the wisps of silver grow in our hair and think of us fondly when we're gone. My identity is just as much informed by the lentil burgers my parents ate on their first date as the sandwiches my boyfriend and I first shared in the Barbican on ours. I often wonder what came first, my love of fried bananas or my love of hearing Nan talk about them.

To cook for - and with - someone you love is such a tangible way to make someone feel you care: when my boyfriend wakes up before me on a chilly morning and I hear the kettle boil and the lever on the toaster lift before I've even realized I want a cup of tea or a slice of toast; when Mum and I take turns in making different layers of a trifle; and when I spritz the last bit of lemon on a fillet of fried fish before my friend takes a bite, that is the love I look for. These are the people that push a glass of water towards your hand when you've drunk too much, bring home your favourite ice cream because you said your day was "just fine", or have a martini mixed and a bowl of chips waiting even before your keys are in the front door. Don't settle for okay-enough food and love that doesn't light you up.

I want you to turn down the corners of these pages with every meal you have in mind. Make the Collapsing Chocolate Cake (*see p.174*) when your father comes over for dinner for his birthday (yes, he will always make jokes about it looking like you dropped it) and bring a pan of Spaghetti Vongole (*see p.44*) straight to the table, balanced between a bottle of white wine, for a long lunch with an old friend. Cook and connect with the person opposite you in the candlelight.

In this book, there are recipes that are super quick to whip up, uncomplicated dishes that taste as though you've spent all day making alongside ones that take a bit of effort, but I promise they won't induce anxiety. There are breakfasts that define the fizz of first love; laid-back lunches for long, lazy days; proper date-night dinners; and desserts and sweet things to be used to signify special times. This book is full of the food you want to cook for your crush when you want to feel fancy. You'll find the dish you want to spend the day sourcing the perfect ingredients so you can cook for your mum on the night you tell her the good news that you've been keeping a secret. There are recipes to choose to make for your first-date dinner that you know you'll want to remember in years to come – a souvenir of when your life began together.

Cooking from this book is all about watching the person you love spoon the panna cotta (that you took hours watching set) into their mouth and smile. Through food we can make a moment as celebratory, as decadent, or as dreamy as we desire. Cook with confidence – what's the worst that could happen? Everything can be saved; walls can be wiped.

Allow food to awaken your senses. Get excited about summer strawberries and look forward to the arrival of winter citrus. Watch tomatoes pop in a frying pan, crusts form on a loaf as it bakes, and cheese melt under a hot grill; everything can be transformed. Step into the kitchen free of fear, don't worry about what could go wrong, be bold, throw in those extra cloves of garlic, be generous with the splash of wine in the pan (and your glass), throw in herbs by the handful and turn the music up as you do it.

These are the recipes to cook when you want to woo someone new with a roast chicken that fills your kitchen with the aroma of hot butter and fresh lemon, just when you need to make someone feel like they're seen. When you look back at your life, it's the time spent, and the food shared, around a table that will mean the most.

Our time together is brief, and real love at times can feel rare. It was this sentiment that was at the forefront of my mind when writing this book; borders were closed and sharing a drink, let alone a meal, with someone I missed seemed far away. Each love story is a multitude of moments married to the food cooked along the way, and with this book I want you to make the recipes your own. Fight for delight in all you eat and with everyone you love.

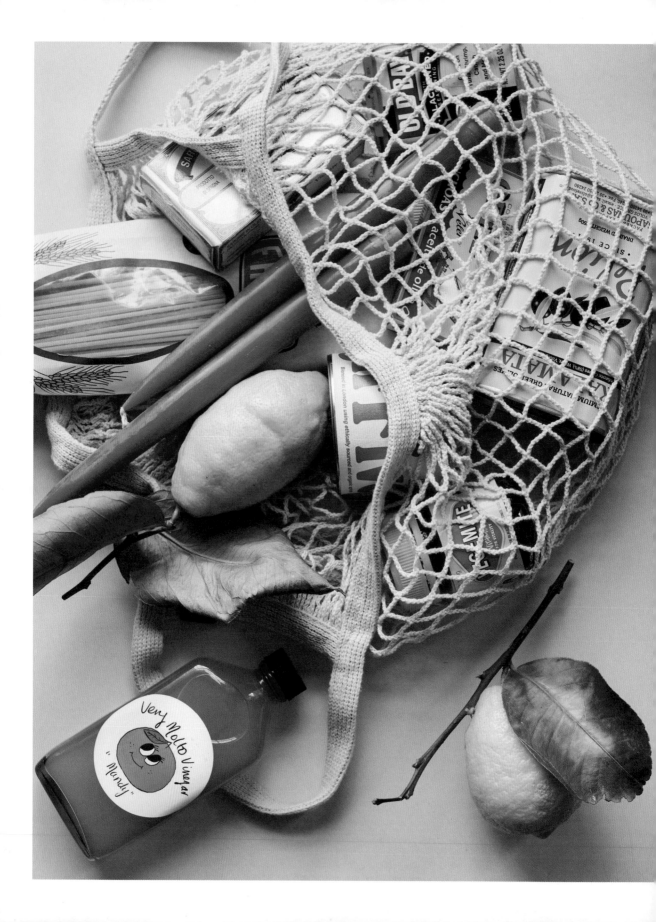

Cook's Notes

*(a few notes to guide you along the way
as you cook through this book)*

Ingredients and Alternatives

- A few of my must dos: I use large eggs at room temperature when baking; I always buy unwaxed citrus fruit as I use the zest in everything; avoid low-fat versions of anything as they really alter the consistency and flavour of what they're added to; and I always use flaky sea salt, unless otherwise specified.

- Cook with the seasons: I'd love you to take these recipes and make them your own. I've made notes throughout where different fruit or vegetables will work, so feel free to change to what you fancy or what's available.

- Taste as you go: for instance, different brands of canned tomatoes will need a pinch of sugar or a drop of vinegar to bring out the sweetness and/or sharpness. Taste as you cook and leave no room for surprises.

Scene Setting

- Start with a clean kitchen, a good playlist, and always have snacks on hand to keep the cook happy.

- Make sure to have a big jug of water, flavoured with slices of lemon or something else lovely, alongside any other drinks you want to serve.

- Above all, don't let fear interfere; everything will be alright when the company is good.

Shapes and Sizes

- I tend to use slightly smaller than standard cake tins, but they're worth getting if you regularly cook for two. It means that no cake is ever wasted, and you'll be surprised how useful a 15cm (6in) cake tin is.

- Pasta shapes are completely interchangeable, depending on your preference. The ones I use in the recipes are my favourite for each dish, but that's not to say I don't love a carbonara with rigatoni.

- All recipes feed two people but certain dishes, especially those that take longer to make or taste even better when left overnight, are made in larger quantities – enough for breakfast or lunch the next day.

Heat and Oven Cooking

- All my recipes are tested in a fan-assisted oven. If you are using a conventional, non-fan-assisted oven, you may need to increase the cooking time.

Part I

EASY TO IMPRESS

Easy to Impress

The dishes within this chapter are for those days when you and your love get home from work weighed down by the world and want to disappear from it all with a bowl of steaming spaghetti and a bottle of your favourite wine. These are the recipes that you'll turn to on the nights when you had forgotten that your best friend, who's just gone through a breakup, is coming over for breakfast and you need to serve a meal that will soothe and say: "everything will be okay". This is a list of what to cook when you want to woo someone, or make them feel special – things to whip up with an ease that looks effortless. They're simple dishes that take no time to make, but look sublime.

Brown Butter and
Sage Scrambled Eggs

When you cook in a kitchen that's not your own, happy accidents can happen. These eggs were one of those, created one sleepy morning when my boyfriend, Joe, and I first started dating and spent every second night switching beds from one side of the Thames to the other. One late Sunday morning in his small South London kitchen, I burnt some butter. I didn't realize how hot his hob (cooktop) could get and, in a flash, the butter was spitting and frothing. The plan was to make us some simple scrambled eggs, but I like to see all accidents as opportunities and this one was no different.

I dug around in his freezer and found a bunch of sage that I had put there the week before, left over from a pasta dish I'd made. I dropped a few of the leaves into the hot butter and watched them sizzle and crisp, just as you would when making a burnt butter and sage sauce for a bowl of ravioli. The butter (and kitchen) was now scented with that unreal fragrance of toasted sage leaves. I let the butter cool a little, then gently added the eggs, and they took on the flavour of the sage-infused brown butter as they softly scrambled.

With just one mistake and a few herbs, this breakfast tasted like we had forked out a tenner for it at a posh cafe around the corner. It takes less than 5 minutes to make, yet once it's topped with a cloud of grated Parmesan and curls of crisp sage, it looks like you could have started making it at sunrise.

---

5 eggs

1 tbsp unsalted butter

6 large sage leaves

sea salt and freshly ground black pepper

hot buttered toast and plenty of finely grated Parmesan cheese, to serve

---

Crack the eggs into a bowl, generously season with salt and pepper and lightly beat with a fork.

Melt the butter in a non-stick frying pan over a medium heat and just as it starts to froth and foam, add the sage and fry until the leaves are crisp and the butter is a deep-golden colour. Carefully remove the sage leaves from the butter and leave them on a plate to one side so they stay crisp.

With the sage-infused butter remaining in the pan, turn the heat to low and after it has cooled for a minute or so, pour in the eggs. Gently stir the eggs until softly scrambled and cooked to your liking.

Season the eggs with a little extra salt and pepper and serve spooned on hot buttered toast with the crisp sage leaves and lots of finely grated Parmesan on top.

Whipped Ricotta Toasts

When I was 16 and newly dating my first-ever boyfriend, my world was awash with the bliss of first kisses and rose-tinted romance. It was like we were the only people on Earth who had ever been in love. One weekend in late summer, we took a six-hour bus ride down the East Coast from Sydney to see our favourite singer play a gig in a small country town. I begged my parents to let me go and they agreed and even let us stay the night in a little bed and breakfast in the town (I think I'd suggested camping, so this seemed like a safer alternative). I had never felt so grown up in my entire life. I can't remember where we went for dinner, what songs the singer sang or much else about that weekend, but I'll never forget the breakfast we woke up to the next morning. This wasn't just a standard B&B, it was run by a couple who I've since learned are famous for their food.

In the early morning summer mist, we sat outside on the terrace of an old house and were served a tray of toast, sliced tomato, pots of thick Greek yogurt, a jar of local honey and fresh ricotta. It was simply the best breakfast I'd ever had. The combination of the hot charred toast and the cold ricotta was so sublime. It's a breakfast I always associate with blue skies and sunshine, and so in summer I now like to whip up big batches of ricotta, either sweet or savoury, to serve on toast throughout the week. I serve either option on a tray so each person can top their own toast. Once whipped, you can keep the ricotta in an airtight container in the fridge for up to a week to eat on toast for breakfast, lunch or dinner.

Savoury Ricotta Toasts

250g (1 cup plus 2 tbsp) ricotta cheese

finely grated zest and juice of ½ small unwaxed lemon

a pinch of sea salt, plus extra to serve

a splash of whole milk

TO SERVE

2 large slices of your favourite bread for toast

1 garlic clove, peeled and cut in half

a few perfectly ripe tomatoes, sliced

1 small bunch of basil, leaves roughly torn

plenty of extra-virgin olive oil

a drizzle of balsamic vinegar

freshly ground black pepper

In a large mixing bowl, add the ricotta, the lemon zest and juice, salt and a splash of milk. Whip the ricotta with an electric hand whisk on high for a few minutes until light and fluffy (or you can do this by hand with a balloon whisk, if you're in the mood). Pop the whipped ricotta in the fridge while you make the topping and toast, or for whenever you want to eat it.

When ready to serve, toast the slices of bread in either a cast-iron griddle pan or under a piping hot grill, so they get slightly charred at the edges.

Rub the cut-side of the garlic over one side of each slice of toast. Spoon some of the whipped ricotta on top, then the sliced tomatoes. Scatter over the basil leaves and finish with a good drizzle of olive oil, a few drops of balsamic vinegar and season with plenty of salt and pepper.

Sweet Ricotta Toasts

250g (1 cup plus 2 tbsp) ricotta cheese

finely grated zest and juice of ½ small unwaxed lemon

1 tsp icing (confectioners') sugar

a splash of whole milk

TO SERVE

2 large slices of your favourite bread for toast

1 handful of walnuts, toasted and chopped

2 tbsp runny honey

a sprinkle of sea salt

In a large mixing bowl, add the ricotta, the lemon zest and juice, icing sugar and a splash of milk. Whip the ricotta with an electric hand whisk on high for a few minutes until light and fluffy (or you can do this by hand with a balloon whisk if you're in the mood). Pop the whipped ricotta in the fridge while you make the topping and toast, or for whenever you want to eat it.

When ready to serve, toast the slices of bread in either a cast-iron pan or under a piping hot grill, so they get slightly charred on the edges. When nicely toasted, spoon the ricotta on top. Scatter over the walnuts and drizzle with the honey, then finish with a little salt.

Peach, Raspberry and Passionfruit Salad

Cold fruit on a hot summer's day is the best way to begin breakfast. However, when I think of fruit salads, what often springs to mind are the sad-looking ones at hotel buffets with anaemic cubes of apple, a small slice of orange and a grape or two, if you're lucky. Fruit salads may not have the best reputation but this one will make you forget all others – I promise. Slices of ripe peach are marinated in the perfume of passionfruit and raspberries. It's the hint of vanilla though that turns this bowl of fruit into something special, and it becomes delightfully jammy as the flavours marry together in the fridge. You can serve the fruit salad by itself or spoon it over thick Greek yogurt, or a bowl of Bircher Muesli.

2 large ripe peaches, halved, stones removed, and sliced

150g (1 heaped cup) raspberries

3 passionfruit, halved

½ tsp vanilla extract

Place the peaches in a large serving bowl and toss in the raspberries.

Scoop out the passionfruit pulp with a teaspoon and add to the bowl. Pour in the vanilla and turn gently until everything is combined. Let sit for 30 minutes or so in the fridge before serving.

Ginger and Apple Bircher Muesli

When I first moved to London for university many moons ago, I'd make a huge batch of bircher muesli on a Sunday night for the week ahead, just so I'd be excited about breakfast and wake up in time for my morning lectures. It worked most of the time, but often resulted in me wanting to linger at the dining table for longer, pondering and then prioritizing my second cup of coffee over finding out the meaning of symbolism in a Virginia Woolf novel.

I've been making the same bircher muesli ever since, spiked with fiery fresh ginger, lots of coarsely grated green apple and vanilla. All it takes to make is a big mixing bowl, a good stir of the ingredients and a night chilling in the fridge. In the morning, just stir again so it becomes really creamy, and maybe add a splash of milk to loosen. I love it served simply as is, or topped with fresh fruit salad and a spoonful of almond butter.

200g (2 cups) whole rolled (old-fashioned) oats

400g (2 cups) Greek yogurt

2 green apples, cored and coarsely grated

½ tsp ground cinnamon

2 tbsp maple syrup

½ tsp finely grated fresh root ginger

a few drops of vanilla extract

3 tbsp apple juice or whole milk, plus extra if needed

In a large mixing bowl, add all the ingredients and stir to combine, then let it sit overnight in the fridge.

When you're ready to serve, stir the bircher again (add an extra splash of apple juice or milk if it looks a little dry) and spoon into 2 bowls.

A Single Rose
on a Table for Two

Every night when I come home and every morning when I leave, I walk past the most exquisitely set table: Pepto-Bismol-pink-hued napkins are folded into ornate shapes and placed between a candle stick and a single-stemmed pink rose, on a small table for two. The table is nestled in an alcove in the restaurant located in the lobby of the building where I live, Oslo Court.

A few years ago, my boyfriend, Joe, and I moved into a tiny 35-square-metre flat on the top floor of this iconic building. We had been looking at places to rent for about 3 months and, as anyone who knows the London rental market, that feels like an eternity of touring some of the most depressing rooms in the city. One day I set the search on the property website citywide just to see if I was missing anything and up popped a place name I instantly recognized.

Oslo Court is a famous art-deco apartment block built in the late 1930s in St. John's Wood, just across the road from Regent's Park. It is famous because it's said to be the only residential building left in London that has a restaurant in the lobby. Oslo Court, the restaurant (named after the building), has been open since the early 1980s and is still run by the same team who haven't made a change to either the decor or the menu since: think pink grapefruit segments grilled with brown sugar and sherry on rose-patterned plates; seafood-stuffed baked crêpes; steak Diane; and a dessert trolley (cart) that's wheeled around by Neil, the black-tie wearing head waiter, who has worked there since the doors first opened.

The average age of the clientele is in their late seventies to early nineties and, from my balcony, I watch them return for anniversaries, birthdays and every occasion worth celebrating. It's the sort of restaurant you go to linger, for dinners that start

with champagne, end with something sweet to sip, and include a bottle or two of wine in between.

Our flat looks over the London skyline and Regent's Park, and when the wind blows in a certain direction it carries the sound of the lions roaring from the zoo nearby. Parakeets and geese from the park fly over the balcony at sunset, and the city's best deli, Panzer's, is just a 5-minute walk away; it's all very romantic. When we first moved in, the rent was slashed to something we could afford because the inside of the flat hadn't been renovated since 1985, and came complete with an original jacuzzi, gold Versace-logo tiles and glass chandeliers that were slightly falling apart. And yet, once we had unpacked and my cat, Joni, was asleep in the sun, it felt like home.

Now, much as I love living here in the faded glamour of the flat, the real romance is the restaurant, because from it I can watch my favourite table, almost like theatre each evening. Every night, I can see a new couple, mother and daughter or old friends, sit and eat by candlelight with the glow of the fuchsia tablecloth beaming through the windows.

In one of my favourite books, *The Table Comes First* by Adam Gopnik, Fergus Henderson (my old boss and the chef and founder of the London restaurant, St. John) comments: "I don't understand how a young couple can begin life by buying a sofa or television. Don't they know the table comes first?" I remember reading this book when I worked at St. John; I was 20 and spent most of my time hungover staring out of the window counting the minutes until the staff lunch bell rang. I read that line and firstly wondered if I'd be one of those young couples one day and, secondly, why the table over a bed? Years later, by the time I was one half of a young couple buying a sofa, a television and, of course, a dining table, I finally understood. I realized that even

"The most important element is, obviously, who you're sharing the table with, the second is what you're eating, and the third is the table itself."

though you can't sleep on it, the table comes first in every relationship across our lives because it's the anchor to everything that really matters. Life happens at the table; it begins and blooms day after day, with every meal we sit down to share. It's where we exchange stories, where conversations that change the course of our lives take place, and where we sip wine and stain tablecloths with spaghetti sauce as we make plans for more nights like this.

The table is the setting for so many scenes throughout my life that have shaped who I am. Evenings spent with my stomach in knots worrying about what the cool-but-cruel girls will say to me at school the next day, calmed by a plate of mashed potato and a pastry-topped pie with my name cut out, made by Mum to make me feel better. Mornings when the Sydney ocean air blew through the windows as I plated up pancakes for my high-school crush, or two-in-the-morning rounds of toast shared still tipsy with my best friend. The intimacy and immediacy of sitting opposite someone, sharing a meal that you've cooked for them, can make you feel you're together in a private universe.

A few months after we moved to Oslo Court in early 2020, the restaurant, like all others across the country, was forced to close. For the following year of lockdowns, it was just my boyfriend and I, and so our table-for-two in our tiny apartment became the centre of our world. In the kitchen with its faded fruit-patterned tiles, chipped worktop and never-ending cupboards, I cooked through all the uncertainty of the world outside. Everything I missed being witness to in the restaurant below, I recreated at our table upstairs while its curtains were closed. I didn't learn how to create elaborate shapes, but I did fold napkins for Sunday lunch, and although my roses were just from the supermarket, I found single stem vases to pop them in. Our days revolved around the comings and goings of the kitchen: from the kettle that whistled before I woke up as Joe brewed coffee; our fried eggs, cereal and crumpet breakfasts shared with the hum of the BBC; lunch eaten together, between Zoom meetings and dinner; and on the balcony we'd watch the sunset no matter the weather. I tried my best not to let the chaos of everything outside puncture the calm we'd created within our walls. As we both worked at the table during the day, the glow of two laptops between us, setting the table for dinner became an important transition.

As a kid it was always my job to set the table, depending on my mood, I'd put placemats the wrong way on purpose and would lay soup spoons instead of forks for spaghetti, but now I see why Mum made me do it. You want to create a table that keeps people there long after the last bite. They have a word for this in Spanish, *sobremesa*, which doesn't really translate into English, but it conveys the time you spend sitting at the table with others long after you've finished your meal. You know those nights when you're newly in love and Saturday evening is spent trying to draw out dinner as long as possible, slowly sipping your glass of wine so you can stay in each other's company a little longer, or those long, holiday lunches when time seems to stop. There's nothing specific that you must do to conjure that feeling of not wanting a meal to end, but there are lots of little things that can help.

The most important element is, obviously, who you're sharing the table with, the second is what you're eating, and the third is the table itself. The romance created with just a single rose, a flickering candle and a freshly pressed tablecloth at Oslo Court may not be new, but it has transformed how I feel about the importance of such frivolous-seeming things. It doesn't have to be elaborate, you don't need a 6-piece cutlery set or different plates for every day of the week, it's all about setting the scene for the anticipation that's about to unfold.

Gathering a few flowers from your garden to set the mood for lunch with your grandmother, or dusting off fancy glassware for your friend's birthday dinner makes the person you're cooking for feel like the meal is as special as they are, even if it's just beans on toast or a bowl of rigatoni that you've whipped up in 5 minutes. As much as I love a cosy dinner where we sit side-by-side on the sofa with bowls of something warm balanced on our knees, there is nothing quite like the feeling of putting on an album, lighting a candle and sitting down together on a table that's ours.

Transform Your Table

(put your phone away and light a candle to signal a shift to a different mood)

1. The tablecloth: a simple one that you found somewhere special or lovingly borrowed from your parent's or grandparent's collection. All being well it will look like a disaster when the dinner is done, but that's the sign of a good meal.

2. The flowers: I'm not fussy about flowers – I like supermarket roses, carnations, tulips and big bunches of green eucalyptus, a reminder of Australia. I think so much of their beauty can be enhanced by how you display them, so I keep my old tiny Campari soda bottles for stunning single roses à la Oslo Court and group bunches of flowers together by shade to create big bursts of colour.

3. The candle: there's something instantly calming about candlelight. I like tall candles in candlesticks, so the light is at face height on the table, bathing you both in that quintessentially romantic glow: tall, plain white candles are effortlessly elegant and cost the least.

4. The cutlery: a fork, spoon and knife per person are all you need. I pick up old cutlery sets on eBay, at markets and in charity shops. Of course, there are fun pieces of cutlery, like cake and oyster forks, steak knives and soup spoons, but they're not essential.

5. The plates and platters: I have risked excess baggage charges on so many trips because I simply can't walk past a plate or platter that I love and not bring it home. From the antique-metal salad dish I found at a flea market in Athens to the plate purchased in the hotel in Paris where we spent a weekend eating strawberries. Nothing matches in my kitchen or at my table, but I wouldn't want it any other way. Find pieces that you love, and you won't ever wish for a matching set of anything.

6. The music: find an album, a playlist, or even a really good radio station to soundtrack your meal.

A Handful of Herbs Omelette

A good omelette can make the best breakfast, lunch or dinner. It can be whipped up in mere minutes and, in my mind, is such a sophisticated thing to serve when done right. Be confident in your omelette skills and I'm sure it'll be a showstopper, and something you'll be asked to make again and again. This one is flavoured with flecks of gorgeous green herbs and salty, sharp cheese and, of course, is cooked in lots of lovely butter.

6 eggs

a handful (1 tbsp each) of finely chopped flat-leaf parsley, tarragon, chives and dill, plus extra to serve if you fancy

2 tbsp double (heavy) cream

2 tbsp finely grated Parmesan or Gruyère cheese, plus extra to serve

30g (2 tbsp) salted butter

sea salt and freshly ground black pepper

Crack 3 eggs into a bowl and add half the herbs, cream and cheese. Season with plenty of salt and pepper and lightly whisk with a fork until combined. Repeat with the remaining 3 eggs, herbs, cream and cheese in a separate bowl.

Melt half the butter in a non-stick frying pan on a medium heat and just as it starts to foam, pour in one of the bowls of the egg mixture. Leave the eggs to cook for about 30 seconds or so until the edges start to set.

Using a spatula, pull the cooked edges towards the centre and swirl the pan so that the raw egg spreads out evenly and fills the space. As the egg sets, gently fold the omelette in half and half again – you can cook it the whole way through or serve it a little runny in the centre, whatever way you fancy. Repeat to cook the second omelette using the rest of the butter and the second bowl of egg mixture.

Serve the omelettes with extra herbs and cheese sprinkled over the top if you're in the mood for more.

Brown Sauce and Marmalade Bacon Sandwich

A good bacon sandwich is a thing of beauty for a hangover. It can turn a rough day around and make you feel like everything is alright. I'm fussy when it comes to bacon sandwiches and have spent literally years and years finessing my method for the best one. My simple rules are that the bacon must be smoked (what is the point of unsmoked bacon?) and it must be as crisp as can be. I cook mine under the grill, which minimizes the mess, rather than in a frying pan, as the bacon becomes more curled and crispy at the edges.

The bacon is coated in a mix of brown sauce, marmalade and mustard, which caramelizes as it cooks and turns the rashers into the most magical thing that's ever been between two slices of bread. It reminds me of the smoky and sweet *bak kwa* (Chinese dried barbecue pork) that I grew up snacking on in Singapore. I can't promise this sandwich will turn your troubles around entirely, but I bet you'll feel a thousand times better after eating one.

6 smoked back bacon rashers

2 tbsp brown sauce

½ tbsp marmalade

½ tsp English mustard

4 slices of white bread

salted butter, for spreading

tomato ketchup, to serve

Turn on the grill to high and lay the bacon on a lined baking tray. Once hot, grill the bacon for about 8 minutes, turning once, until cooked and most of the fat has rendered but it's not yet crisp. (Drain the fat and keep it to fry your eggs or make fried rice another time.)

Meanwhile, in a small bowl, mix the brown sauce, marmalade and mustard. Brush the sauce over both sides of each bacon rasher, then grill until crisp. Keep an eye on the bacon to make sure it doesn't burn – it should take about 2 minutes on each side.

You can toast the bread under the grill or just pop it in the toaster. Butter each piece of toast and sandwich together with the bacon – 3 rashers each – and serve with ketchup on the side, if you fancy.

Soda Bread With Whipped Butter

Have you ever woken up to the aroma of freshly baked bread? There really is nothing better. Keep this page of the book open and place it on the pillow of the one you love so they get the hint to make it for you, or make a batch yourself and give them the best morning wake up. As much as I've tried to get into sourdough, I don't have the patience and so I'll forever stay a soda bread sort of lady. Soda bread comes together in a matter of minutes, and within half an hour of waking you could be spreading whipped butter onto a slice of warm bread that you've baked that morning.

As I love a chewy crust, I cut the dough into 4 rolls, so you get a greater surface area, but you can make a single loaf. A combination of buttermilk, bicarbonate of soda (baking soda) and vinegar help to make the crumb lovely and light. I always make sure I have wholemeal (whole wheat) spelt flour in the cupboard for this bread, but if all you've got to hand is plain flour, just use that. I make soda bread at least once a week and the spelt flour gives it a deep savoury flavour, which I adore.

While I could write a whole book about my love of bread, one of the best things about it is that it's a vehicle for butter, and special bread deserves special butter. Making a batch of whipped butter at home feels as though you could be in a fancy restaurant – light as lace, the butter is made to be generously spread, so don't be shy.

SODA BREAD

125g (scant 1 cup) wholemeal (whole wheat) spelt flour, plus extra for dusting

125g (scant 1 cup) plain (all-purpose) flour

1 tsp bicarbonate of soda (baking soda)

¼ tsp fine sea salt

250ml (1 cup plus 1 tbsp) buttermilk

1 tsp runny honey

1 tsp white wine or cider vinegar

WHIPPED BUTTER

250g (2 sticks) salted butter, softened

a sprinkle of sea salt flakes

LEFTOVER WHIPPED BUTTER

You'll have plenty of leftover whipped butter: try it spooned over a stack of warm pancakes; as a dip for crunchy radishes; or spread over your morning slice of toast.

Heat the oven to 180°C fan (400°F/Gas 6) and line a baking tray with baking (parchment) paper. Sprinkle an extra handful of spelt flour over a chopping board.

Sift both types of flour, the bicarbonate of soda and salt into a large mixing bowl, then stir until evenly combined.

In a small bowl, mix the buttermilk, honey and vinegar. Pour the buttermilk mixture into the dry ingredients, then use your hands to mix it into a dough, bringing everything together quickly and scooping in the flour mixture from the sides of the bowl. It will be quite a wet dough once it comes together.

Tip the dough out of the bowl onto the floured board. Shape into a round, then using a sharp knife, cut it into 4 even-sized, triangular-shaped rolls. Place the rolls on the lined baking tray, evenly spaced apart.

Dust the top of each roll with extra flour and bake for 25 minutes, until golden brown and cooked through.

While the bread is baking, make the whipped butter. Place the butter in a large mixing bowl and whip with an electric hand whisk on high for about 10 minutes, until pale and fluffy. Spoon the butter into a serving bowl and sprinkle over a little sea salt flakes. Set aside.

Serve the soda bread warm from the oven with the whipped butter on the side and your favourite marmalade, jam, honey or cheese.

The All-Day Breakfast

(hope for your hangover)

Wake up late on the weekend: juice some oranges; brew a pot of coffee; make this breakfast; and I promise everything will feel brighter.

Sweet-and-Sour Beans • Thyme-Butter Mushrooms and Tomatoes • Sausages and Bacon • Fried Eggs • Toast

---

The first meal I ever ate in London was a fry-up: beans, black pudding (blood sausage), mushrooms, tomatoes, plus a fried egg, and bread so buttery I imagine it was probably also fried. It was all piled high on a platter in a cafe tucked down a side street next to Trafalgar Square. It's somewhere my dad had been going since he first moved to the city in the '80s, and later a place I found out that my boyfriend, Joe, also went to for his hungover breakfasts in his early twenties. I was 14, visiting London for the first time, and feeling heartbroken after being let down by a high-school crush. I had arrived after a 24-hour flight from Sydney – listening to my iPod full of sad songs on repeat as I sobbed underneath a dusty aeroplane blanket – a fry-up was just what I needed. When we sat down on the small, orange-plastic chairs, Dad ordered for me and the ultimate fry-up soon arrived. It really was a dish that felt like love, every element cooked to perfection and coming together to make a meal so complete it would be a joy any time of the day.

When I moved to London years later, I realized the cafe was just down the road from my old

university, so if feeling homesick in between lectures, I'd walk down and sit for hours with a notebook, order a fry-up and endless cups of tea. It's been a landmark of my life ever since, a place I've returned to with a hangover, a heart beyond broken, and for hope on days when London didn't yet feel like home. It's now where Joe and I go together when we've drunk too much wine on the weekend.

I know nothing beats a greasy-spoon fry-up, nothing at all, but on the mornings when one isn't in reach, this is my version. The beans take less than 30 minutes and while they're simmering away, you can make a start on the rest of the meal, then fry the eggs just before you serve. This menu has a method in that it's all about starting things in a frying pan and finishing them in the oven. The mushrooms, tomatoes, sausages and bacon are crisped up in the pan, then cooked through in the oven so that you're making the most of your time and getting the best flavour and texture possible from each component.

Sweet-and-Sour Beans

Spicy, sweet and a little sour, these beans are so good that you could skip the rest of the menu and just spoon them onto 2 slices of buttered toast and be done with it. They have that quintessential *agrodolce*, sweet-and-sour balance, that I adore and look for in so many of my recipes. Use whatever white beans you can get your hands on, I prefer buying jarred ones as I think the flavour is a little better than canned, but if you want to go above and beyond, use soaked dried beans and cook them in stock beforehand. You could also double the recipe and make a stash for your freezer, so the next time you wake up and regret that last martini, breakfast is almost ready.

1 tbsp olive oil

1 small red onion, finely sliced

a pinch of sea salt

2 garlic cloves, finely sliced

1 tbsp tomato purée (tomato paste)

½ tsp dried chilli flakes (crushed red pepper flakes)

1 tbsp maple syrup or runny honey

1 tsp Worcestershire sauce

½ tsp smoked paprika

450g (drained weight) jarred or canned white beans, such as butterbeans/lima or cannellini, whatever you fancy, rinsed

1 bay leaf

1 tsp vinegar (any sort will do but balsamic adds a lovely layer of sweetness)

Heat the olive oil in a large, heavy-bottomed pot over a medium heat. Add the onion and salt and cook for about 5 minutes, until translucent. Add the garlic and tomato purée, stir, and cook for 1 minute, until fragrant. Stir in the chilli, maple syrup or honey, Worcestershire sauce and smoked paprika.

Tip in the beans and stir to coat them in the spiced onion mix. Add 200ml (scant 1 cup) water and the bay leaf, stir, and simmer for 20 minutes on a medium heat with the lid on. Halfway through, stir the beans, using a wooden spoon to crush some against the side of the pot to thicken the sauce. Turn the heat off and stir in the vinegar and a little more salt if needed. Serve in the pot at the table.

Thyme-Butter Mushrooms and Tomatoes

While they may not seem like the main event in a proper fry-up, if you spend a little bit of time preparing the mushrooms and tomatoes, they become the star of this breakfast. They're started off in a frying pan in a little butter until golden and caramelized before going into the oven to slowly roast, which gives them an incredible depth of flavour, and allows you carry on with the rest of the breakfast.

15g (1 tbsp) salted butter

a pinch of ground nutmeg

½ tsp dried thyme

2 plum tomatoes, cut in half

2 large Portobello mushrooms, stalks trimmed

plenty of freshly ground black pepper

a pinch of sea salt

a few flat-leaf parsley leaves, to finish

Heat the oven to 180°C fan (400°F/Gas 6) and get a large baking tray ready for all the elements of your breakfast. (Your beans should be simmering away at this stage.)

In a large frying pan, melt the butter with the nutmeg and thyme over a medium heat.

Turn the heat up to high and add the tomatoes, cut-side down, and the mushrooms, stalk-side up, to the pan and cook for 5 minutes, until they start to turn golden and caramelize. Transfer the tomatoes and mushrooms to the baking tray.

Grind over plenty of black pepper and sprinkle with the salt before popping the tray in the oven for 20 minutes while you carry on with the rest of the menu. Scatter the parsley over before serving.

Sausages and Bacon

If you want to keep this menu vegetarian, skip this stage or use veggie sausages, but read on if you're thrilled by the idea of a bacon-scented kitchen on a weekend morning. For me, bacon simply must be smoked. While for bacon sandwiches, I like back bacon, for a fry-up I want the irresistible crunch of streaky bacon. Choose whatever sausages you prefer, I like Cumberland with their mix of mace, nutmeg and sage.

2–4 of your favourite sausages

4 smoked streaky bacon rashers

Don't bother wiping the pan that you've cooked the mushrooms and tomatoes in, all that flavour is going to add to your sausages and bacon. Cook the sausages first in the hot pan for about 10 minutes, until they're golden all over. They don't need to be cooked all the way through, but as soon as they've got a great colour all over, place on the baking tray in the oven with the mushrooms and tomatoes and cook for another 10 minutes.

Follow the same method with the bacon, first crisping it up in the pan, then finishing it off for 5 minutes in the oven.

Fried Eggs

If you fancy, you can use the fat rendered from the bacon to fry your eggs; they will be brilliant and super crispy. However, if you're skipping the bacon, pop a bit of butter in the pan before frying. The eggs will only take 2–3 minutes, so leave them until just before you're about to serve the whole breakfast.

salted butter, for frying (optional)

2 eggs

a sprinkle of sea salt

plenty of freshly ground black pepper

Crack the eggs into the hot pan, containing either the bacon fat or the butter, so they instantly crisp up on the bottom.

Add a splash of water and pop the lid on for a minute to cook the whites through, while leaving the yolks runny. They will take 2–3 minutes to cook in total. Season with the salt and pepper.

TO SERVE

Make some toast for two.

Take the baking tray out of the oven with the roasted mushrooms and tomatoes, super-crispy bacon and sausages. Pile everything onto 2 plates and add the eggs.

Place the pot of beans in the middle of the table and both brown and red sauce, of course.

Serve the breakfast with fresh orange juice and a huge mug of tea or coffee.

Twice-Baked Potatoes With Mackerel, Mustard and Herbs

Ignore the title of this book for just a minute as some meals demand to be eaten on the sofa. Baked potatoes are a dinner to be savoured with a blanket on your lap as someone pours you a glass of something good, placing it next to you as you press play on the millionth re-watch of your favourite film. I make this for dinner for us both at least once a week in winter. It's the most comforting thing to cook because once you pop the potatoes in the oven, you don't have to do anything for an hour, then when they're done you just scoop the inside out and stir in the already-cooked ingredients.

I use smoked mackerel, here, because it's the cheapest smoked fish I can find at my local, terribly stocked supermarket, but smoked sardines, haddock or trout are ideal too. Smoked fish can be a little salty, so stir the fish into the mashed potatoes, taste, then season with salt if needed. Serve the baked potatoes with a crisp salad dressed in a lemony vinaigrette and mustard to match.

2 large baking potatoes

a drizzle of olive oil

90g (6 tbsp) soured cream or crème fraîche

1 tsp wholegrain mustard

2 tbsp chopped parsley or dill (or both!)

3 spring (green) onions, finely chopped or 2 tbsp chopped chives

a little finely grated unwaxed lemon zest

⅛ tsp freshly ground nutmeg

plenty of freshly ground black pepper

100ml (6½ tbsp) whole milk

150g (5½oz) smoked mackerel or whatever smoked fish you can find

1 handful of coarsely grated mature Cheddar, Parmesan or Gruyère cheese

a sprinkle of sea salt

Heat the oven to 200°C fan (425°F/Gas 7). Rub the potatoes with a drizzle of olive oil and a little salt, then bake for about 1 hour, until cooked through. Take the potatoes out of the oven but leave it on.

Slice each potato in half crossways, scoop the soft potato inside into a large mixing bowl. Put the potato skins on a baking tray.

Add the soured cream or crème fraîche, mustard, herbs, spring onions or chives, lemon zest, nutmeg, pepper and milk to the bowl, then mash everything together until smooth.

Peel the skin off the mackerel, roughly flake the fish and gently fold it through the mashed potato mix, taking care not to break it up too much. Taste for seasoning and add salt or extra pepper and/or lemon zest if needed.

Spoon the mackerel mix into the potato skins and sprinkle over the cheese of your choice. Bake the potatoes for a further 15 minutes, until the tops are crisp and golden. Serve with a crisp green salad and mustard.

Chilli-Jam Clams

This bowl of clams is so quick and so simple, yet it looks and tastes spectacular. Shellfish is always impressive and clams are, without doubt, my favourite. Small and sweet, they work so well with lots of chilli, garlic and wine. A good jar of chilli jam does a lot of the work here. Choose one that you'd like to use on other things (I love it smeared on a cheese sandwich) and as long as it's super spicy it'll work wonderfully. The dish takes less than 20 minutes to prepare, so makes an excellent starter or light lunch served with grilled bread. Sharing a big bowl of hot clams and a bottle of chilled wine would be on my list of five favourite ways to spend an afternoon, so may I suggest you give it a go too.

800g (1¾lb) clams

2 tbsp olive oil

1 tbsp chilli jam

2 garlic cloves, finely grated

120ml (½ cup) dry rosé wine

¼ tsp finely grated unwaxed lemon zest

2 tbsp finely chopped flat-leaf parsley, plus extra to serve

1 tbsp salted butter

sea salt and freshly ground black pepper (optional)

Start by cleaning your clams. Tip them into a colander and rinse well. Sort through the clams, discarding any with broken shells or that won't close tightly when tapped on the worktop. Add the clams to a big bowl of fresh cold water and soak for 10–20 minutes, changing the water once or twice, to remove any sand in the shells, then scoop the clams out of the water and into a bowl.

In a large, heavy-bottomed pot, add the olive oil, chilli jam and garlic and let them sizzle for a minute or so over a medium heat until fragrant. Add the clams and stir to coat them in the garlic-spiced sauce.

Pour the wine into the pan and instantly pop the lid on to let the clams steam open in the wine. Take the lid off after 4–5 minutes, give the clams a stir, then put the lid back on but take the pan off the heat.

Let the clams sit for another 5 minutes, then add the lemon zest, parsley and butter and stir again. It shouldn't need any salt as the clams will already be salty, but taste and see if it needs a little seasoning.

Spoon the clams and any sauce in the pan into a large serving bowl and scatter with a bit more parsley. Serve with grilled crusty bread to mop up the spicy sauce.

Prawn and Pistachio Tagliolini

There is a pathway that runs along the coast of the Ligurian Sea, near the Italian city of Genoa, named after Anita Garibaldi, a Brazilian republican revolutionary and wife of Giuseppe Garibaldi. It is said to be one of the most romantic walks in the world. It's also a pathway that I've spent a lot of time on, eating gelato, jumping off rocks into the sea, and walking between our hotel and whichever restaurant we've chosen to eat in.

I first visited this part of Italy on a work trip and have returned every year since, on or around my birthday in August. There's something so special about this stretch of coastline; sometimes I think I love it so much because it reminds me of where I grew up in Sydney, with its rock pools and coastal walks, but really the main reason I return is for the food – Ligurian basil, Ligurian olive oil and seafood from the Ligurian Sea are second to none.

On one holiday for my birthday, I did my research and booked a restaurant recommended to me by a local guide, who had helped me as a translator on my first trip. With my broken Italian, I booked over the phone and didn't think about it again until we were getting dressed for dinner. Google Maps told me it was a twenty-minute stroll down the Anita Garibaldi pathway along the ocean. When we got to the restaurant, we saw what can only be described as a shack painted to look like an old German pub – not quite the authenticity or beauty I was looking for in a fancy birthday dinner.

Since we had booked unfashionably early, we were the only ones there and, before the menus arrived, we muttered to each other that maybe I'd made a mistake and it was one of the stunning seafront restaurants that we had just walked past. But once the menu arrived and I saw a pasta dish with prawns and pistachios – a Sicilian slant on Genoa's famous pesto – I knew we were in the right place. Now, before I even book flights to Genoa, I make sure I book a table at this restaurant. This is my re-creation of that dish, which is packed full of good olive oil, basil and perfumed pistachios. I use ready-made pistachio butter, but you can make your own by blitzing roughly a cupful of whole nuts in a food processor until smooth and creamy. Paired with delicate strands of tagliolini pasta, this dish is something special.

250g (9oz) dried tagliolini, or other long, thin pasta such as angel hair
1 huge handful of fresh basil leaves
2 tbsp pistachio butter
60ml (4 tbsp) extra-virgin olive oil
1 tsp sea salt
juice of 1 lemon
200g (7oz) raw prawns (shrimp), peeled and deveined
1 tsp salted butter
2 garlic cloves, crushed
freshly ground black pepper

Cook the pasta in a big pot of boiling salted water following the packet instructions. Just before draining the pasta, scoop out a mugful of the cooking water and save.

While the pasta cooks, in a blender or food processor, blitz the basil leaves, pistachio butter, olive oil, salt and lemon juice until smooth.

Cut each prawn in half lengthways so that when you twirl the delicate strands of pasta, you'll be able to get both prawn and pasta on your fork. Melt the butter in a sauté pan on a medium heat, add the garlic and prawns and cook for 3–4 minutes, until the prawns turn pink.

Pour a little of the pasta cooking water into the basil and pistachio mix and blitz again until combined.

Add the drained pasta to the sauté pan with the basil and pistachio mix and toss together with the prawns and a little more of the pasta water, if needed. Pile the pasta high on 2 plates to serve and season with black pepper.

Spaghetti Vongole

One of the best things to share with someone over a long summer lunch is a platter of spaghetti and clams. At a restaurant on the southern Italian island of Ischia a few years ago, my Mum and I sat by the water's edge and watched little anchovies swim past as we waited for what was rumoured to be the best spaghetti vongole around. It arrived at the table still in the huge metal pot that it was cooked in, adorned with a handful of parsley and a little fresh red chilli – it was a thing of true beauty. With tongs, we divided it between our bowls and took our time finding every clam in the bottom of the pot until we were sure there were none left.

It was a long lunch and the pot of clams was so good we went back the next day, and the one after that, to order it again and again. Every time I've made spaghetti vongole since it has been in a bid to capture the feeling of that first lunch again. It's the sort of dish that reminds me of warm sunshine and chilled white wine. It leaves you with a messy olive oil-stained tablecloth and garlic-scented fingers, but I wouldn't want it any other way. Bring it to the table still in its pot for the full Ischian effect.

1kg (2¼lb) small clams

250g (9oz) dried spaghetti

60g (4 tbsp) unsalted butter

4 tbsp olive oil

3 large garlic cloves, thinly sliced

½ medium-hot red chilli (chile), deseeded and finely chopped (leave the seeds in, if you fancy more heat)

finely grated zest of ½ unwaxed lemon

100ml (6½ tbsp) dry white wine

1 big handful of flat-leaf parsley, roughly chopped

juice of 1 lemon

sea salt and freshly ground black pepper

Start by cleaning your clams. Tip them into a colander and rinse well. Sort through the clams, discarding any with broken shells or that won't close tightly when tapped on the worktop. Add the clams to a big bowl of fresh cold water and soak for 10–20 minutes, changing the water once or twice, to remove any sand in the shells, then scoop the clams out of the water and into a bowl.

Cook the spaghetti in a big pot of boiling salty water for 2 minutes less than instructed on the packet.

Meanwhile, in a large, heavy-bottomed pot, heat 3 tablespoons of the butter and 3 tablespoons of the olive oil on a low heat, slowly letting them come together. Once the butter has melted, add the garlic, chilli and lemon zest and let it infuse for a minute or so.

Just as the kitchen starts to fill with the scent of everything gently sizzling, turn the heat up and pour in the wine. Let the wine reduce a little, then add the clams and give them a quick toss in the buttery garlic wine. Pop the lid on the pot and cook the clams for 4–5 minutes, until the shells open.

Taste the sauce from the clams to check if you need to add salt, it all depends on how salty the clams are, and season with pepper. When the pasta is about 2 minutes away from being fully cooked, scoop out the spaghetti with tongs and add it to the pot of clams. Toss the spaghetti with the clams and parsley, then pop the lid on and let the spaghetti absorb the broth for a few minutes.

Add the remaining butter and olive oil and the lemon juice and toss together a final time, then bring the pot to the table. All there's left to do is to pile the spaghetti vongole into 2 bowls.

Carbonara

Would I cook carbonara for dinner every night in my dream world? Yes, absolutely, undoubtedly, but I think I would live in a constant state of heartburn. This dish is rich, this dish is decadent, and that's what makes it so perfect. In the film version of the imitable Nora Ephron's novel, *Heartburn*, Meryl Streep's character gets up in the wee hours of the morning to whip up a carbonara for her new lover, played by Jack Nicholson. Two forks, two people, one bowl, one bed – could a first date end any better? Every time I rewatch that scene, I think of one of my favourite quotes on love by the Irish writer, Anne Enright, "*Love is a great punishment for desire.*"

Heartburn is perhaps a worthwhile punishment for both love and carbonara. It's not an everyday dish, but that's why it's so good. It feels fitting for those first moments in a new relationship when everything small really matters; it's the world of first things shared. It's a time in love when there are seemingly no consequences – you could eat carbonara for dinner seven nights a week, and not crave anything green.

Carbonara is fast, just five ingredients thrown together with some care, which is handy as you don't have to leave your guest alone for too long before you return with a feast. Mine is a classic-ish version, no cream, of course, but I can't resist the warmth a little nutmeg brings.

250g (9oz) dried spaghetti

85g (3oz) pancetta or guanciale if you can get your hands on some, diced

1 whole egg

2 egg yolks

35g (½ cup) finely grated pecorino cheese

35g (½ cup) finely grated Parmesan cheese

a pinch of freshly grated nutmeg

a tiny pinch of sea salt, plus extra to cook the pasta

plenty of freshly ground black pepper

Cook the spaghetti in a big pot of boiling salted water following the packet instructions.

Meanwhile, cook the pancetta or guanciale in a dry sauté pan over a medium-high heat until crisp and golden. Take the pan off the heat and remove half of the rendered fat from the meat (save to use in another dish).

In a bowl, combine the whole egg and yolks, cheese, nutmeg and season with a tiny pinch of salt and plenty of pepper.

Just before the spaghetti is ready, add a small ladleful of the pasta cooking water to the egg mix and whisk quickly to combine.

Using tongs, scoop the spaghetti out of the pot into the pan of pancetta, add the egg mixture and cook briefly over the lowest heat, tossing until every strand of pasta is evenly coated in a glossy sauce. Serve immediately with an extra sprinkle of cheese.

Artichoke and Black Pepper Fettuccine

Spending time in Rome in April just as artichokes come into season is possibly the most spectacular place to be. I try to go every year around Easter when it's hot enough during the day for gelato, but not too full of crowds like it can be in the summer. I know it's a city with beautiful tourist attractions, like the Trevi Fountain and Spanish Steps, but, to me, the most stunning thing to see is the man in Campo de' Fiori market lovingly preparing artichokes.

It is a vegetable that requires a little patience, attention and dedication to prepare. Patience is not a virtue I usually possess, so most of the time when I cook artichokes at home, they come from a jar. This dish is a tangle of glossy strands of fettuccine coated in a sauce inspired by two of Rome's most revered pasta dishes, carbonara and *cacio di pepe*. The sauce is rich and silky, thanks to the addition of egg and an extra egg yolk, and features a plentiful amount of toasted black pepper, which brings warmth to the sweetness of the artichokes. It's a meal that doesn't need much cooking since once the pepper is fragrant and the artichokes a little golden, you just toss the hot pasta through the sauce before serving.

200g (7oz) dried fettuccine

---

1 tsp freshly ground black pepper

---

1 tsp salted butter

---

2 garlic cloves, finely sliced

200g (7oz) jarred or canned artichokes (drained weight), roughly chopped

---

50g (1¾oz) Parmesan or pecorino cheese, finely grated, plus extra to serve

---

1 egg

---

1 egg yolk

---

1 tbsp finely chopped basil, plus extra to serve

---

a pinch of sea salt, plus extra to cook the pasta

Cook the fettuccine in a big pot of boiling salted water following the packet instructions.

Meanwhile, add the black pepper to a large cold, dry pan and toast on a medium heat until fragrant. Don't let the pepper burn, so just as it starts to smell nice and toasty, stir in the butter and garlic. Let this all sizzle for a minute before adding the artichokes. Stir and let the artichokes catch a little colour for a minute or so before turning off the heat.

As the pasta cooks, whisk together the Parmesan or pecorino, egg, egg yolk, basil and a pinch of salt. About a minute before the fettuccine is done, scoop out a small ladleful of the cooking water and stir it into the egg mix.

Drain the pasta and keep a mugful of the pasta cooking water to one side. Add the pasta to the artichokes in the pan and, on a very low heat, pour the egg mix over. Toss together until every strand of fettuccine is coated in the smooth, glossy sauce, adding extra pasta water, if needed.

Serve the pasta piled into 2 bowls with more basil and finely grated Parmesan.

Chickpea and Pomegranate Salad

I used to take a container of this salad to school in my lunchbox. It was a salad Mum became famous for when we lived in Singapore and every time she made it, she was asked for the recipe. It's hard not to love – chickpeas paired with pomegranate and herbs tossed together in a sweet-and-sour dressing of syrupy pomegranate molasses and savoury tahini. I serve it alongside the baked feta with flatbreads for a light lunch.

400g (14oz) can chickpeas, drained and rinsed

1 pomegranate, quartered and seeds removed

1 small cucumber, finely chopped

1 small bunch of mint, leaves finely chopped

1 small bunch of parsley, leaves finely chopped

½ red onion, finely diced

2 tbsp red wine vinegar

1 tbsp pomegranate molasses

4 tbsp extra-virgin olive oil

1 tbsp tahini

sea salt and freshly ground black pepper

In a large mixing bowl, add the chickpeas, pomegranate seeds, cucumber, mint, parsley and red onion.

In a small bowl, whisk together the vinegar, pomegranate molasses, olive oil and tahini. Season with salt and pepper to taste. Pour the dressing over the salad and toss together just before serving.

Baked Feta With Honey and Thyme

Anything that resembles a present, feels like a gift and this baked feta is no exception. Combined with honey, thyme and chilli, the feta is wrapped in a baking (parchment) paper parcel and tied with kitchen twine. I love feta in all forms, but when it's baked it has the most incredible texture and really takes on any flavours that you cook it with. You can serve the feta as a side dish alongside grilled meat, vegetables and salad, or spread generously over grilled toast for something more substantial – either way, bring it to the table still warm and wrapped and let your guest open the parcel.

200g (7oz) block of feta

1 tbsp runny honey

1 tsp thyme leaves

½ tsp dried chilli flakes (crushed red pepper flakes)

Heat the oven to 180°C fan (400°F/Gas 6).

Take the feta out of its packaging and pat it dry with kitchen paper. Lay the feta in the middle of a sheet of baking (parchment) paper, about three times the size of the cheese, then place it on a baking tray.

Spread the honey over the top of the feta and sprinkle with the thyme and chilli.

Loosely fold the sides of the paper over the feta, then fold in the ends like a present and secure with kitchen twine. Bake for 30 minutes, or until you can smell the fragrance of the honey and thyme when you open the oven door.

Untie the kitchen twine at the table and open the parcel, taking care of the hot steam as you do. Serve straightaway.

Anchovy and Walnut Dip With Crudités

If it's very hot in London sometimes the only thing I want to make is this dish. It can be cooked in one pan in mere minutes, then you just need to slice some raw vegetables to serve with it. It is inspired by a version Joe and I ate on a date to Spring, the gorgeous Skye Gyngell restaurant in London's Somerset House, on a very hot summer's night after one too many cocktails on the Southbank and a dreamy walk over Waterloo Bridge. We were so hungry by the time we sat down and this was the first dish to arrive – it's one neither of us has stopped thinking about since.

The dip is served warm and is the sort of savoury thing you crave alongside a drink before dinner, or as a starter to something larger. Based on an Italian *bagna cauda*, a blend of anchovies, garlic and herbs from Piedmont, this version has a coarser texture and uses olive oil, not butter, and lots of deep-green parsley. You can choose to serve it with whatever raw vegetables you fancy, but radishes, carrots and fennel are my favourite. Alternatively, spoon the dip onto toasted bread; it's also divine with burrata, drizzled over a pizza or even as a pasta sauce.

---

your favourite mix of crunchy raw vegetables, like radishes, radicchio, endive, carrots and fennel

100g (¾ cup) walnuts halves

50g (1¾oz) can anchovies in olive oil, about 6–8 fillets

3 garlic cloves, finely grated

¼ tsp dried chilli flakes (crushed red pepper flakes)

finely grated zest and juice of 1 unwaxed lemon

100ml (6½ tbsp) extra-virgin olive oil

3 tbsp finely chopped flat-leaf parsley

a pinch of sea salt

freshly ground black pepper

First prep your vegetables, trimming them and/or slicing into sticks, if needed, then arrange on a platter ready to serve.

Toast the walnuts in a dry frying pan over a medium heat, turning once, until deeply fragrant and darker in colour. Set aside to cool.

Tip the anchovies into a small pan with the oil from the can and let them sizzle on a medium heat, stirring, until melted into the oil.

Take the pan off the heat and pour the anchovies and their oil into a mini food processor (or you can use a pestle and mortar). Add the toasted walnuts, garlic, chilli, lemon zest and juice, olive oil and parsley. Blitz or grind briefly to a coarse-textured dip. Season with a pinch of salt, if needed, although the anchovies should be salty enough, and black pepper.

Pour the dip into a small bowl and serve warm with the crudités on the side.

Clerkenwell Rarebit

During my first 8 years in London, I lived in a neighbourhood called Clerkenwell.
A short walk from St. Paul's Cathedral, Shoreditch and Bloomsbury, it was the
centre of my world and I rarely wanted to leave. My street was bookended
by an almost medieval meat market on one end that ran from midnight to 6am
throughout the week and a farmer's market at the other that opened all weekend.
Clerkenwell was traditionally the Italian quarter of the city, like the suburb I'm from
in Sydney, and there were many Italian delis at that time. Terroni of Clerkenwell was,
and still is, my favourite deli in the area; it has every pasta shape you can imagine,
cheese, and cured meats swinging from the ceiling, and Italian football blasting from
the television at all hours of the day.

This recipe is influenced by the famous Welsh rarebit from St. John (which
reminds me of my twenties and a dish I ate almost every Friday night for all of
8 years) combined with the best Italian cheese, Taleggio, my must-have weekend
buy from Terroni. It's a dish to make when you want your cheese-on-toast
dinner to feel a little fancier.

---

1 tbsp unsalted butter

2 tbsp plain (all-purpose) flour

120ml (½ cup) dry white wine

85g (3oz) Taleggio cheese, rind removed
and chopped into small pieces

20g (¼ cup) finely grated Parmesan cheese

60g (2oz) mozzarella cheese, drained
and torn into pieces

a pinch of ground nutmeg

2 slices of sourdough bread

sea salt and freshly ground black pepper

crisp green salad, to serve

Melt the butter in a small pan over a low heat, then stir in the
flour. Using a balloon whisk, mix the butter and flour together
to make a paste, then keep stirring until it starts to smell toasty.

Pour the white wine into the pan and whisk vigorously for
a few minutes until smooth and thickened to the consistency
of white paint. Add the Taleggio, Parmesan and mozzarella
and stir until the cheese has melted and the sauce is smooth.
Stir in the nutmeg, then season with salt and pepper. Pour into
a bowl and chill the cheese topping for 3–4 hours, until firmed up.

Turn the grill to high. Line a baking tray with baking (parchment)
paper. Toast both sides of the bread and spread the cheese
topping evenly over one side of each slice. Place on the lined
baking tray and grill until golden in places and bubbling. Serve
with a crisp green salad.

Rainbow Chard, Polenta and Ricotta

This is one of my favourite weeknight meals to make, no matter the time of year. It's perfect for those days when you want a big bowl of something green to eat, but have no desire for salad. I have an affinity for anything that combines hot and cold elements in one bowl, and a spoonful of the hot, cheesy polenta with the cool, mellow ricotta and the warm green leaves of the marinated chard never misses.

1 large bunch of rainbow chard, about 400g (14oz) in total, stalks thinly sliced and leaves roughly chopped

finely grated zest of ½ unwaxed lemon

juice of 1 lemon

1 garlic clove, minced

1 litre (4⅓ cups) stock, either chicken or vegetable

250g (1⅔ cups) quick-cook/instant polenta (cornmeal)

a splash of whole milk (optional)

1 tbsp salted butter

150g (5½oz) Parmesan cheese, finely grated

125g (4½oz) ball of mozzarella cheese, drained and torn into pieces

a pinch of freshly grated nutmeg

100g (½ cup minus 1 tbsp) ricotta cheese

a drizzle of extra-virgin olive oil

sea salt and freshly ground black pepper

Put the chard into a large pan, pour in enough water to just cover and cook over a high heat until the stalks are tender and the leaves wilt. Drain and place in a bowl.

While the chard is cooking, mix the lemon zest and juice with the garlic. Season with salt and pepper, then pour the dressing over the chard while it's still warm and leave to marinate.

In a pot, bring the stock to a simmer, then slowly pour in the polenta, beating continuously with a balloon whisk for 5 minutes, until thick, smooth and no longer grainy. Add a little milk or water if it becomes too thick – it should have a soft, spoonable consistency. Add the butter, Parmesan, mozzarella and nutmeg and give the polenta a good stir to combine everything – the mozzarella should melt and become gorgeously gooey. Taste and add salt and pepper, if needed.

Pour the soft polenta into 2 serving bowls and top with the lemon and garlic chard before adding generous dollops of ricotta. Drizzle with olive oil and eat immediately before the polenta starts to set.

OTHER LEAFY GREENS

If rainbow chard isn't in season, switch it for any leafy green, or frozen spinach. For something different, try sautéeing mushrooms in a little butter and thyme until golden, or roast a roughly chopped aubergine (eggplant) with garlic and honey until soft on the inside and caramelized on the outside, then pile it on top of the polenta.

A Summer
Sunset Dinner

Make the most of the glut of glorious end-of-summer produce with an al fresco supper, best eaten under pink evening skies.

Stuffed Fried Olives • Courgette and Lemon Risotto • Peach, Pistachio and Mozzarella Salad • Intensely Apricot and Amaretti Ice Cream

---

I spent a lot of summers in London wanting nothing more than to fall in love. Back in the years when I was single, I thought a summer without romance was a waste: I wanted a big love to spend long, hot days and enjoy afternoons in the pub with; or to join me on train trips to the coast. Six summers came and went before any real romance revealed itself, but looking back, they weren't a waste; love was there, just in disguise.

There were summers spent cooking with my best friend, Maddi, when, both hopelessly without direction, we'd make elaborate meals to feel we at least had one part of our lives sorted. It was the time of the year that Mum would come over from Sydney and she'd cook for me using the produce she missed during the winter in Australia:

aubergine (eggplant) fried in gram flour, finished with a drizzle of hot honey; or lamb grilled on my tiny barbecue to eat alongside salads of tomato and handfuls of fresh herbs.

Summer in London is fleeting, you catch glimpses of it throughout the season, but on days when it really shows off, there's nothing more glorious. Yes, risotto requires lots of stirring but it comes together quick enough, and once you see it spooned into bowls flecked with ribbons of courgette (zucchini) flowers, it's worth every second of standing at the stove. You can breadcrumb the olives, whip the ice cream, and blitz together the salad dressing in advance, so all you have to do on the day is fry the olives, make the risotto and assemble the salad and scoop the ice cream.

Stuffed Fried Olives

Something salty, fried and finished with a spritz of fresh lemon is just how I want to start a meal. These olives are first stuffed with Gorgonzola and parsley, then coated in breadcrumbs and fried until golden and crisp on the outside and soft inside. I buy them pre-pitted as they're easier to stuff than trying to remove the pits yourself.

45g (1½oz) Gorgonzola cheese, cut into 12 small pieces

¼ tsp roughly chopped parsley

12 large green olives, pitted

2 tbsp plain (all-purpose) flour

1 egg, lightly beaten

50g (1 heaped cup) panko breadcrumbs

250ml (1 cup plus 1 tbsp) flavourless oil, such as sunflower

sea salt

1 lemon, cut into wedges, to serve

Put the Gorgonzola on a plate, sprinkle the rosemary over, then turn the cheese to coat it in the herb. Stuff the middle of each olive with a piece of parsley-coated Gorgonzola.

Put the flour, the egg, and the breadcrumbs in separate shallow bowls. Dust each olive in the flour, then dunk it into the egg, followed by the crumbs until evenly coated. Repeat until all the olives are coated.

Heat the oil in a heavy-bottomed pan over a medium heat – it's at the correct temperature when a breadcrumb dropped into the hot oil sizzles and turns light golden. Fry the olives in batches of four for 3–4 minutes, until golden and crisp, then drain on kitchen paper (paper towels).

Sprinkle the olives with salt and serve with wedges of lemon for squeezing over.

Courgette and Lemon Risotto

Risotto will always hold a special place in my heart. I love the different adaptations I make throughout the year, from pumpkin or mushroom in the autumn to pea and broad bean in the spring. One risotto I can't wait to make each summer is this, with its electric-orange ribbons of courgette (zucchini) flowers, mint and lots of lemon.

700ml (2¾ cups) vegetable or chicken stock

1 tbsp olive oil

½ white onion, finely chopped

a pinch of salt

1 courgette (zucchini), finely sliced

2 garlic cloves, minced

230g (2¼ cups) arborio rice

120ml (½ cup) dry white wine

finely grated zest of 1 unwaxed lemon

1 tsp thinly sliced mint leaves

25g (¾ cup) finely grated Parmesan cheese

4–6 courgette (zucchini) flowers, finely sliced

1 tbsp unsalted butter

Pour the stock into a big pot and when it starts to simmer take it off the heat.

Meanwhile, in a large sauté pan, add the olive oil, onion and salt and cook over a medium heat for 3–5 minutes, until the onion is soft and translucent.

Add the courgette (zucchini) and sauté, stirring, for another 5 minutes, until tender. Add the garlic, let it sizzle for a minute, then stir in the rice, coating each grain in the olive oil mixture.

Pour the white wine into the pan and stir until absorbed by the rice. Add the hot stock, a ladleful at a time, stirring until each spoonful is absorbed. Continue until all the stock has been added and the grains of rice still have a little bite, but aren't crunchy. It should take about 20 minutes in total.

Take the pan off the heat and stir in the lemon zest, mint, Parmesan, courgette flowers and butter. Cover and leave for 5 minutes to let the flavours mingle. Meanwhile, make the peach and mozzarella salad.

Peach, Pistachio and Mozzarella Salad

I love the perfume of a ripe peach with the soft creamy mozzarella and nutty sweetness of pistachios, these three ingredients would be good no matter how you use them. You gently blitz the pistachios in the vinaigrette to emulsify some of them into the dreamiest dressing. Make sure to use really ripe peaches – the juice should run down your knife as you cut into them; when a peach is perfect, there is nothing better.

2 tbsp shelled unsalted pistachio nuts

2 tbsp extra-virgin olive oil

1 tbsp lemon juice

a generous pinch of salt

2 peaches, halved, stones removed and sliced

125g (4½oz) ball of mozzarella, drained and roughly torn

1 small handful of basil leaves

sea salt and freshly ground black pepper

In a blender, add the pistachios, olive oil, lemon juice and salt, then blitz for a few seconds, pausing occasionally, until the dressing is creamy with a few pieces of pistachio.

Arrange the peach slices and mozzarella on a platter and spoon the pistachio dressing over.

Scatter basil leaves over the salad and season with salt and pepper, to taste.

Intensely Apricot and Amaretti Ice Cream

Homemade ice cream requires a bit of effort, but it's a worthwhile endeavour. This one is not made in a fancy machine, but just with a hand whisk. Roasting the apricots first gives them a marzipan-sweet intensity, and as they caramelize in the oven. I fold crumbled amaretti biscuits through the ice cream at the end to add texture and to lift the note of almonds.

300g (10oz) ripe apricots, halved and stones removed

1 unwaxed lemon

3 green cardamom pods, split

3 tbsp caster (superfine) sugar

200ml (scant 1 cup) double (heavy) cream

200ml (scant 1 cup) condensed milk

a pinch of salt

1 tsp vanilla extract

100g (3½oz) crisp amaretti biscuits, crumbled, plus extra to serve

Heat the oven to 180°C fan (400°F/Gas 6). Place the apricots, cut-side up, in a roasting dish and top with a slice of lemon peel, the cardamom pods and a splash of water. Sprinkle the sugar over evenly. Roast the apricots for 30 minutes, until they start to caramelize in places, then leave to cool.

Remove and save the cardamom seeds, then discard the cardamom pods and lemon peel. Purée half of the apricots with the cardamom seeds in a blender. Roughly chop the rest of the apricots.

In a large mixing bowl, whip the cream with an electric hand whisk until soft peaks form. Fold the condensed milk, apricot purée and chopped apricots into the whipped cream with the juice of the lemon, the salt and vanilla. Whisk again until a pale-yellow cream. Fold through the crumbled amaretti, then spoon into an airtight container with a lid and freeze for 4 hours.

Decant the ice cream into the mixing bowl and whisk until extra light. Return to the container and freeze for another hour – it should be like a soft gelato. Scoop into dishes and serve with extra crushed amaretti on top.

Smoked Chilli and Vodka Rigatoni

If you have a bottle of vodka, a tube of tomato purée (tomato paste) and some cream, you're very close to creating a plate of pasta akin to pure bliss. This is the sort of meal you want to eat after one too many glasses of wine. It's carby, creamy and super spicy. The sauce is greater than the sum of its parts and comes together in the time it takes to boil the pasta. The classic combination of garlic and onion is the root of many sauces, but here they're finely grated to add a base note to the intensity of the sweet tomato purée and richness of the cream. The vodka mellows any hint of acidity to create a real star of a sauce. The best part though is the smoked chilli – just a teaspoon shifts this to the sort of dish you want to cook 5 nights a week, and continuously crave.

250g (9oz) dried rigatoni

15g (1 tbsp) unsalted butter

½ white onion, finely grated

a pinch of sea salt, plus extra to cook the pasta

4 garlic cloves, finely grated

3 tbsp tomato purée (tomato paste)

1 tsp smoked dried chilli (chile) flakes

75ml (5 tbsp) vodka

100ml (6½ tbsp) double (heavy) cream

1 handful of basil leaves, finely sliced, plus extra leaves to serve

1 handful of freshly grated Parmesan cheese, plus extra to serve

Cook the rigatoni in a big pot of boiling salted water following the packet instructions.

While the pasta is cooking, melt the butter in a deep sauté pan over a medium heat. Add the onion and sauté with a pinch of salt for about 5 minutes, until softened. Add the garlic and cook, stirring, until fragrant, then add the tomato purée and smoked chilli flakes. Turn the heat down a little, stir and cook gently for 2 minutes.

As the tomato paste caramelises and starts to darken in colour and stick to the bottom, pour in the vodka and stir to deglaze the pan. Let the vodka cook off and reduce before stirring in the cream. The sauce should be smooth, creamy and deep orange in colour. Stir in the basil and Parmesan.

Drain the rigatoni, reserving 4 tablespoons of the pasta cooking water. Add the pasta and cooking water to the sauce and toss to combine.

Serve the pasta topped with extra basil leaves and grated Parmesan or, for a total delight, a ball of burrata. Eat immediately and enjoy.

SMOKED CHILLI FLAKES

If you can't find smoked chilli or chipotle flakes, use regular dried chilli (crushed red pepper flakes) and add a tiny pinch of sweet smoked paprika instead to give that gorgeous smoky flavour.

Honey Chorizo and Pea Toasts

Things on toast will have my heart forever and it was a food category that my late grandfather, Barry, had a particular fondness for. No matter what was left over from dinner the night before, be it spaghetti Bolognese or a plate of roast potatoes, he would pile it high on generously buttered toast for breakfast the next day. His appetite for a big breakfast is something I've definitely inherited. This is a dish that I make intentionally, not just to use up leftovers; it comes together in about 15 minutes, but feels like a substantial snack, light lunch or starter.

You can use whatever bread you fancy – sometimes I like to serve the topping on small discs of toasted baguette for a canapé-style starter or on thickly cut sliced sourdough when I want to make a meal of it. The honey completely transforms the chorizo, coating it in a gorgeous caramel that pairs so well with the sweetness of the peas and sharp lemon. I use frozen peas most of the time, but when they're in season, I love podding fresh peas.

200g (1½ cups) fresh or frozen peas

3 tbsp crème fraîche

¼ tsp finely grated unwaxed lemon zest

a generous pinch of sea salt, plus extra to cook the peas

plenty of freshly ground black pepper

2 tsp finely chopped mint, plus extra leaves to finish

100g (3½oz) chorizo sausage, sweet or spicy up to you, skin removed, cut into 2cm (¾in) thick slices

1 tsp runny honey

1 garlic clove, peeled and left whole

toasted sliced bread of your choosing, such as baguette or sourdough

Cook the peas in a small pan of boiling salted water for about 5 minutes, until tender. Drain and immediately immerse the peas in a bowl of iced water to cool.

In a mixing bowl, mix the crème fraîche, lemon zest, salt, pepper and chopped mint.

Drain the peas, pour half into a blender or mini food processor and blitz to a coarse purée. Spoon the puréed peas and the whole peas into the bowl with the crème fraîche mix and stir to combine.

Fry the chorizo in a dry frying pan on a medium heat until crisp, and the fat has rendered. Take the pan off the heat, stir in the honey to coat the chorizo.

Slice the end off the garlic clove and rub it over the hot toast. Spoon the pea mixture onto the toast and top with the honeyed chorizo, then finish with extra mint leaves and a drizzle of the spicy honey oil from the pan.

The Pleasure
of Pre-Made Pizza

(an ode to Ina's ethos)

On the third finger of my left hand, I have a small, raised scar from a knife that slipped. I was 23 and had run home (quite literally) to spend my lunch break preparing dinner for a man I thought I was falling in love with. It was the first time he'd come over for a proper dinner and I'd decided I wanted to cook something extravagant. Over the months that we had been seeing each other, I had secretly logged the flavours he loved the most, and then tried my best to squeeze them all into one meal. So, the night before the dinner, I stayed up late to make delicate little pots of panna cotta topped with a layer of electric-pink rhubarb jelly, and covered a joint of pork with fennel seeds and plenty of salt.

On the day of the dinner, I sprinted from my office near St. Paul's back home to Clerkenwell to get some more prep done in my lunch hour, so that when he arrived that evening it looked like I had just whipped up the dinner with ease. As I sliced an onion to place under the pork, the knife slipped and cut my finger. I burst into tears, wrapped the finger and kept slicing. By the time I had put the pork in the oven to slow cook and was back at my office desk, I received a text from him asking if we could move the dinner to the next day. Tears ensued again and I spent the evening alone in my flat, which was now scented with roasting onions and apples, and ate a pre-made pizza and drank a bottle of wine.

Now, just imagine instead of all that fuss, I'd just ordered a pizza for our dinner together? So often, when I'm standing in my kitchen or writing notes about what to cook, I catch sight of the scar and think, don't fuss, store-bought is fine.

I know this is a cookbook and I'm a food writer, but sometimes the best thing you can do is pick up a pizza that you've had nothing to do with the creation of. I'm a devotee of American author Ina Garten's ethos, "store-bought is fine". I have idolized the cookery writer and television host since I was a kid living in Singapore, watching her on Food Network. As she waltzed from her breezy Hamptons kitchen to her gorgeous garden to grill something for her and husband Jeffrey's dinner, I was in awe of her ease, because Ina makes everything look effortless.

Growing up I noticed my family adopted a similar philosophy to Ina's "store-bought is fine". If Mum cooked an impromptu lunch for her friends, she'd drive to our local Chinese takeaway, buy a crispy roasted duck and serve it tossed through a green salad with fresh lychees and a gingery dressing. My nan's lemon cake, that I loved so much, scented with huge lemons from the tree in her garden, is a vanilla cake mix with lemon juice and zest stirred through before baking. Sometimes shortcuts can be the main event.

You'll never see me making puff pastry, laminating the dough with layers of butter; an ice-cream maker doesn't fit in my cupboards; and I have yet to even see a sourdough starter near my kitchen. Instead, I concentrate my efforts on things that I know always taste better homemade, because nothing is worth depleting yourself for; it must be fun – cooking must be a pleasure.

On the days when it's not and you're not feeling it, but still want to create something beautiful for someone, the store-bought saviours opposite will come to the rescue. Keep them in your freezer, hide them at the back of your kitchen cupboard for a rainy day and never run home in your lunch break to cook for someone who probably has already forgotten how you take your tea.

My Essential "Store-bought-is-fine" List

(the things I turn to when I don't feel like cooking)

- Find a packet of your favourite shop-bought ravioli and top it with something that takes the same time to make. I love pumpkin and amaretti ravioli served with a little crispy sage and brown butter; or mushroom ravioli topped with fresh mushrooms sautéed in lots of olive oil and garlic.

- I have been known to arrive at a friend's house with a jar of orange juice and Grand Marnier already mixed and a packet of pre-made crêpes. I make the sauce from the Crêpes Suzette recipe *(see p.164)* and they turn out close to perfect. Once something is soaked in booze and caramel, there's little room for error.

- Buy a ready-made lemon tart and top it with fresh raspberries; if you're feeling super fancy, pipe raspberry jam into each raspberry and place them on top of the tart in any pattern that your heart desires. If it's a birthday, I've been known to use raspberries to write out numbers.

- Yes, roasting a chicken is a lovely thing to do on a Sunday *(see p.139)* but a supermarket rotisserie chicken is in my eyes the best thing since sliced bread. Use it in soups, salads, and sandwiches.

- A sheet of puff pastry can be turned into many things, so I always have one stashed in my freezer. Spread the pastry with a jar of black olive tapenade, then top with canned anchovies and very finely sliced onion. A sprinkle of thyme, a little ground black pepper and 40 minutes in a hot oven later and you're done – a tart to be proud of.

- If when hosting a breakfast or brunch, all you can manage is to pour orange juice into glasses and make some coffee – then that's fine. Frozen croissants and pain au chocolats may not be as perfect as heading down to your local bakery, but smelling them fresh from the oven feels like you've made an effort.

Pici with Roasted Tomatoes, Olives and Anchovies

My kitchen cupboards can hardly cope with my cocktail glass collection, let alone a pasta machine, so these hand-rolled pici are my shape of choice when I want to make pasta at home. They're not perfect, but that's how I like them. Each long noodle is unlike anything you can buy, and they are such fun to make together. Divide the dough in half and see who can master the pici roll. They take mere minutes to cook, and the sauce is equally as easy to make since the tomatoes, olives and anchovies are roasted together in the oven.

PICI

300g (2 cups) 00 flour, plus a handful for dusting

½ tsp fine sea salt

1 egg and 1 egg yolk, beaten together

75g (½ cup) fine semolina

finely grated Parmesan cheese, to serve

ROASTED TOMATO SAUCE

300g (2 cups) mix of small tomatoes on the vine

5 garlic cloves, skin on

4 tbsp olive oil

4 anchovy fillets in oil, drained

2 tbsp small green and black olives, pitted

a pinch of dried chilli flakes (crushed red pepper flakes)

a pinch of sugar (optional)

sea salt and freshly ground black pepper

Start by making the pici. Tip the flour in a pile on a clean work surface, or in a large mixing bowl, make a well in the middle and sprinkle over the salt. Add the beaten egg and 6 tablespoons of water to the well and bring it all together with your hand to form a scraggly dough. Knead the dough for 10 minutes, until a smooth ball, then wrap and chill for a few hours, or overnight if you fancy.

An hour or so before you want to roll and cook the pici, make the roasted tomato sauce. Heat the oven to 160°C fan (350°F/Gas 4). Add the tomatoes on the vine, garlic, olive oil, anchovies, olives and chilli to a large roasting tin, mix to combine, and roast for 1 hour, until the tomatoes have caramelized and started to burst. Take the tin out of the oven, pop the garlic out of its skin and pull the tomatoes off the vine. Roughly stir everything together, crushing some of the tomatoes and mashing the garlic. Taste the sauce for seasoning: depending on your anchovies it may need a little more salt, and depending on your tomatoes it may need a tiny pinch of sugar.

While the tomatoes are roasting, start to roll the pici, dust a clean work surface with flour. Pinch off small walnut-sized pieces of the dough, then roll them in your hands, or on your kitchen countertop, into a long worm shape. Roll them as long and thin as you can – it doesn't matter if they're not even, just have fun with it.

Sprinkle the semolina over a baking tray and lay the rolled pici on the tray, spacing them slightly apart so they don't stick together, as you work your way through the dough.

Put a big pot of salted water on to boil and just before you add the pici give them another roll in your hands to even them out a little. Boil the pici for about 3 minutes, until they float to the surface of the water.

Drain the pici, add to the roasting tin and toss with the warm roasted tomato sauce until combined. Serve topped with plenty of finely grated Parmesan.

Easy to Impress

Chicken and Courgette Piccata

This is a one-skillet dinner that tastes like it has taken hours to make. It's also one of my favourite things to cook as the number one fan of capers, and look for anything to include them in. Here, sweet and salty capers are paired with lots of lemon juice, lemon slices (buy a big bag of lemons for this dish as you'll need plenty), mustard, white wine and garlic to create a sauce that's so good you'll want to put it on everything. I also wanted to find a way to cook not just the chicken but the vegetable element of the meal too, so thinly sliced coins of courgette (zucchini) simmer away with the tender pan-fried cutlets of chicken along with slices of lemon, which become divine and jammy over time. I like to serve the piccata on top of mashed potato (with lots of butter and nutmeg) or with a crusty loaf, so not one drop of the sauce goes to waste.

2 skinless, boneless chicken breasts

30g (2 tbsp) unsalted butter

70g (½ cup) plain (all-purpose) flour

100ml (6½ tbsp) lemon juice, about 3 lemons in total

100ml (6½ tbsp) dry white wine

1 heaped tbsp capers, drained

2 garlic cloves, finely grated

1 tsp Dijon mustard

1 large courgette (zucchini), thinly sliced into rounds

½ unwaxed lemon, cut into paper-thin slices

3 tbsp double (heavy) cream

sea salt and freshly ground black pepper

a few flat-leaf parsley leaves, to finish

Take the chicken breasts out of the fridge about 20 minutes before you start so they're not too cold and to ensure a lovely golden colour when they are fried. On a chopping board, slice each chicken breast in half lengthways through the thickest part to give 4 evenly sized pieces. Season the chicken with salt and pepper, then place a sheet of baking (parchment) paper on top. Using a rolling pin or similar, bash the chicken to flatten to about half as thick, roughly 2cm (¾in).

Melt the butter in a large frying pan on a high heat until a deep golden brown.

Put the flour in a shallow dish and generously season with salt and pepper. Dust each chicken breast piece in the seasoned flour and place in the hot butter. Fry the chicken for 2–3 minutes on each side, until it has a golden crust.

While the chicken is frying, mix the lemon juice, wine, capers, garlic and mustard in a small bowl ready to make the sauce. When both sides of the chicken are golden, take the pieces out of the pan and place on a plate. It doesn't matter if the chicken is not fully cooked at this stage as it will be heated through again in the sauce.

Add the courgette (zucchini) and lemon slices to the pan and sizzle for a few minutes until they catch some colour and start to caramelize. At this point, pour in the wine and lemon juice mix and simmer for a minute or so until the citrus scent fills your kitchen.

Put the chicken back in the pan, add the cream and give it a stir. Turn the heat to low, pop on the lid and simmer for a final 5 minutes. At this point, the sauce should have thickened and reduced a little and the chicken will be infused with the lovely flavour of the sauce. Sprinkle over the parsley and serve.

A Holiday When the Sky is Grey

Ignore what the weather is doing outside, light some candles, put on a Dean Martin album, and share a platter of seafood spaghetti; summer and the sea will feel closer than you think.

**Burrata With Honey-Roasted Fennel, Olives and Rosemary •
Bitter Leaves With Blood Orange and Crispy Crumbs • Seafood Spaghetti
• Perfumed Panna Cotta**

When it's cold outside, the sunshine feels far away, and all you want is a holiday, make this menu and you'll feel one step closer to summer. It conjures up the scent of the sea, no matter where you are cooking it, and centres around a platter of spectacular seafood spaghetti.

I love to make this menu for Valentine's Day in London. Mid February in the city always feels a bit grim and grey, so Valentine's is a real light in an otherwise cold, rainy month. As I watch people coming home from work on the tube clutching bunches of red roses and elegant ribbon-tied boxes of chocolate, I'm heading home with a parcel of paper-wrapped seafood from my fishmonger, Steve Hatt, which is my version of romance. Cooking this menu at home feels just as special as going out for dinner; you also don't have to worry about being rushed out of the restaurant to make room for the next sitting, allowing you and your love to linger over the spaghetti, open another bottle of wine, dance to your favourite music, and make plans to share a bowl of pasta again sometime soon.

This is a menu inspired by the gorgeousness of seasonal winter produce. At the start of February as my local greengrocer fills up with Italian blood oranges, lemons with their leaves, and bright-pink forced rhubarb from Yorkshire, I instantly feel like winter is on its way out. Combined with ingredients like rosewater and bay leaves (the things in my cupboard that transport me somewhere sunnier in an instant), this is a meal that transforms your kitchen.

A few tips about planning ahead: it's best to make the panna cotta the night before, or the morning of the dinner so it has time to set and chill. Enjoy the burrata with honey-roasted fennel while the pasta sauce simmers away, and your meal will all come together nicely.

Burrata With Honey-Roasted Fennel, Olives and Rosemary

Burrata is perfect with just a drizzle of gorgeous green extra-virgin olive oil and a little sea salt. That said, when served like this it becomes a plate of pure pleasure; the cool stracciatella cream in the middle of the burrata when paired with the warmth of the honey-roasted fennel and olives unites my favourite hot-and-cold combination. Serve on its own or with some garlic-brushed grilled bread, so you don't miss a drop of the herb-infused olive oil.

1 fennel bulb, thickly sliced, fennel fronds reserved

1 tbsp runny honey

a big pinch of sea salt, plus extra to serve

3 tbsp olive oil

½ tsp finely grated unwaxed orange zest

½ tsp dried chilli flakes (crushed red pepper flakes)

1 ball of burrata, about 125g (4½oz)

1 large rosemary sprig

1 handful of green olives

Heat the oven to 160°C fan (350°F/Gas 4). Line a large baking tray with baking (parchment) paper. Place the fennel on the lined tray.

In a small bowl, mix the honey, salt, half the olive oil, the orange zest and chilli flakes, then pour it over the fennel. Turn to ensure the fennel is evenly coated, then roast for 35 minutes, until tender enough to pierce with a knife and the honey marinade has caramelized around the edges. Let the fennel cool a little.

Meanwhile, take the burrata out of the fridge so it isn't too cold when served, drain and place on a serving plate.

Heat the rest of the olive oil in a small pan on a medium-high heat. Add the rosemary sprig and green olives and fry until fragrant and slightly crisp.

Arrange the fennel around the burrata and spoon over any of the honey marinade in the baking tray. Spoon the hot olives and crispy rosemary over the burrata. Top with the delicate bright-green fennel fronds and an extra sprinkle of sea salt.

Bitter Leaves With Blood Orange and Crispy Crumbs

A good salad has to have something sweet, something crunchy, something bitter, and something soft – this salad has it all.

1 head of radicchio, leaves roughly torn

1 head of endive, thinly sliced

1 blood orange, peeled

CRISPY CRUMBS

15g (1 tbsp) salted butter

2 garlic cloves, finely grated

50g (1 cup) panko breadcrumbs

2 tbsp finely grated Parmesan cheese

a sprinkle of sea salt

DRESSING

½ tsp Dijon mustard

½ tsp runny honey

3½ tbsp extra-virgin olive oil

a big pinch of sea salt

½ tsp white wine vinegar (optional)

plenty of freshly ground black pepper

Start by making the crispy crumbs. Melt the butter in a small frying pan on a medium heat. Stir in the garlic and fry until it just starts to sizzle. Add the breadcrumbs and fry for about 5 minutes, turning occasionally, until golden and crisp. Let the crumbs cool in the pan, then stir in the Parmesan and season with salt.

In a large serving bowl, toss the radicchio with the endive. Segment the orange over a small bowl that you'll mix the dressing in, so that you save as much of the juice as possible.

To finish the dressing, add the mustard, honey, olive oil and salt to the small bowl containing the orange juice and whisk to emulsify. Taste the dressing – it may need the vinegar, but it all depends on how acidic the blood orange is. Pour the dressing over the leaves and toss together to combine. Top with the orange segments and sprinkle over the crumbs, to serve.

Seafood Spaghetti

A word of warning: don't wear white when eating this; it's a dish that has the ability to destroy tablecloths and clothes as you twirl the pasta and fight forks over who gets the last prawn. It's centred on two things that make me feel euphoric no matter their context – seafood and spaghetti – which come together in a fragrant tomato sauce scented with fennel seeds, bay and lemon. I add just the tiniest pinch of cinnamon and quite a bit of chilli to really make me feel like I'm eating it on a beach in Sicily.

For the sauce, you gently simmer the squid for 1 hour, until it's tender and butter soft. I promise that all fears of rubbery squid will be calmed once you eat this. I was taught to slowly braise squid by food writer and academic, Rebecca May Johnson, and have never looked back. As you pop your spaghetti on to boil, the prawns poach and the mussels steam open in the rich tomato sauce. Have a platter and 3 bowls waiting, one for each of you and one to pile the empty shells into.

2 tbsp extra-virgin olive oil, plus extra for drizzling

½ white onion, finely chopped

a pinch of sea salt, plus extra to cook the pasta

3 garlic cloves, finely sliced

1 tsp dried chilli flakes (crushed red pepper flakes)

½ tsp fennel seeds

2 tsp tomato purée (tomato paste)

1 unwaxed lemon

1 bay leaf

2 x 400g (14oz) cans chopped tomatoes

200g (7oz) squid, cleaned and sliced into rings

a pinch of sugar

a tiny pinch of ground cinnamon

250g (9oz) dried spaghetti

200g (7oz) mussels, scrubbed and cleaned

100g (3½oz) raw prawns (shrimp), peeled and deveined, tails left on

1 handful of flat-leaf parsley, roughly chopped, plus extra to serve

Heat the olive oil in a very large, heavy-bottomed pot on a medium-high heat. Add the onion and salt and let it sizzle for a minute or so. When the onion has started to soften and turn translucent, turn the heat down a little and add the garlic, chilli, fennel seeds and tomato purée. Stir and let it sizzle for a minute or so until you can smell the aroma of each ingredient.

Using a potato peeler, peel a large strip of zest from the lemon and add this to the pot with the bay leaf. Just as everything starts to caramelize, pour in the chopped tomatoes. Use a wooden spoon to scrape the bottom of the pot and stir it all together. Pour in 200ml (scant 1 cup) water and add the squid.

Turn the heat down as low as it will go and simmer the sauce for 1 hour, stirring every now and then to make sure it doesn't stick to the bottom. After 1 hour the sauce will have reduced and the squid will be soft and tender. Sprinkle over the sugar to taste and add the cinnamon.

Cook the spaghetti in a large pot of boiling salted water for 2 minutes less than instructed on the packet. Five minutes before the pasta is ready, give the tomato sauce a stir and add the mussels and prawns to the pot. Turn the heat up to medium, pop the lid on and cook for 5 minutes, until the mussel shells open and the prawns turn pink.

When the spaghetti is almost fully cooked, scoop it out with tongs and add to the seafood sauce with a small ladleful of the pasta cooking water, then toss everything together with the heat still on.

Add the parsley and the juice of ½ lemon, then leave the lid on the pot for a few minutes to allow the spaghetti to absorb the sauce. Remove the lid and give the dish another toss together. Drizzle with extra olive oil and transfer the seafood spaghetti to a serving platter. Scatter over extra parsley.

Perfumed Panna Cotta

Delicate and divine, perfumed with vanilla and rose, these little panna cotta are utterly irresistible. They have a luxurious, voluptuous wobble, and are equally lovely served by themselves as they are with the roasted rhubarb on the side. If you can't get your hands on a vanilla pod, a good-quality paste will work too. These panna cotta are super simple to make, but do start to prepare them either the night before, or the morning of serving to allow them time to chill and set.

200ml (scant 1 cup) double (heavy) cream

3½ tbsp whole milk

1 vanilla pod, split and seeds scraped out, or 1 tsp vanilla paste

60g (4 tbsp) caster (superfine) sugar

1½ sheets of gelatine

½ tsp rosewater

2 rhubarb stalks, trimmed and chopped into equal-sized pieces

a little finely grated orange zest

juice of 1 orange

crystallized rose petals, to decorate (optional)

In a small pan, gently warm the cream, milk, vanilla and 3 tablespoons of the sugar on the lowest heat for 10 minutes, until infused. Stir occasionally to ensure the sugar dissolves and does not stick to the bottom of the pan. Take the pan off the heat.

Add the gelatine to a large bowl of cold water and let it soak for a few minutes until soft. Remove the gelatine from the water and stir it into the warm milk mixture with the rosewater until dissolved.

Pour the mix into 2 x 125ml (½ cup) moulds or small glasses. Pop them in the fridge where they'll need about 6 hours or so to fully set.

Heat the oven to 160°C fan (350°F/Gas 4). Place the rhubarb in a baking dish and sprinkle over the remaining sugar, the orange zest and juice. Roast the rhubarb for 15 minutes, until tender but it still holds its shape. Set aside to cool completely.

To serve, gently dip the moulds or glasses into warm water to help ease the panna cotta out onto serving plates. Serve with the rhubarb and, if you're feeling fancy, a single crystallized rose petal placed on top.

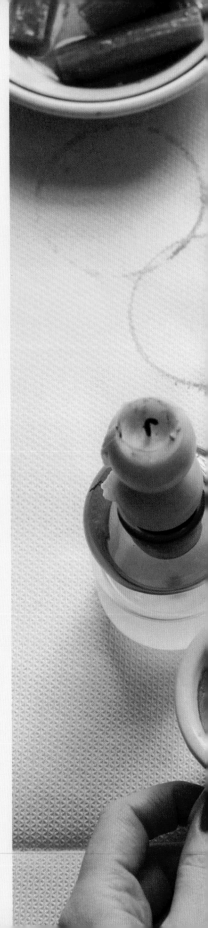

A Slice of Summer

There is no need to dust off the ice cream maker or even whip cream for this recipe, it is a weeknight, throw-it-together sort of dessert that still looks like you've spent the summer learning how to make gelato. All it takes is two tubs of your favourite vanilla ice cream and some berries. It'll be happy in your freezer for up to a month, so you can treat yourself to a slice whenever you fancy. The ice cream needs no adornment, but I also like to serve it with the rum-spiked Drunk Chocolate Sauce (*see p.178*).

2 x 450g (1lb) tubs of vanilla gelato or ice cream

100g (1 cup) strawberries, hulled

juice of ½ lemon

75g (½ cup) frozen raspberries

Put the tubs of ice cream in the fridge about 1 hour before you want to assemble everything to let the ice cream soften.

Meanwhile, line the base and sides of a 900g (2lb) loaf tin with baking (parchment) paper – it's easier to line the tin if you wet the paper first, scrunch it into a ball, then unfold before using.

Blend half the strawberries with the lemon juice in a blender until smooth (you can pass the purée through a sieve to remove the seeds if you're fussy, but I tend to skip this step as it's one less thing to wash up). Chop the rest of the strawberries into small bite-sized pieces.

When the ice cream has softened, scoop one of the tubs into a mixing bowl and fold in the puréed strawberries until combined and pale pink in colour, then fold in the chopped strawberries. Pour the strawberry mix into the bottom of the lined loaf tin in an even layer, then freeze.

Spoon the second tub of ice cream into a mixing bowl and crumble in the frozen raspberries. Stir to combine and ripple the raspberries through the ice cream. Spoon the raspberry ice cream on top of the strawberry layer in the loaf tin, spread evenly and freeze for 3 hours, until both layers are completely set.

When ready to serve, turn the ice cream out of the loaf tin, then run a heavy-bladed knife under hot water to make it easier to slice.

Madeleines

Cooking in my mum's kitchen is considerably more fun than cooking in my own; she has all the gadgets and tools I could ever dream of. Cake tins imprinted with lace-like flowers, so they turn out ready decorated, and every apple slicer, cherry pitter, serving tray size or soy sauce saucer you could ever need. I cause chaos every time I go home, ransacking the cupboards to look for new things to cook with. In this chaos, sometimes things vanish, much to Mum's chagrin, and each year, I come back with something from her kitchen. I like having her things with me in my London kitchen – they remind me of her and are the tools that taught me to cook.

The first thing I "borrowed" when I moved out at 18 was a madeleine tray. One of my earliest memories was buying it with her in Paris in the early '90s at Galeries Lafayette. It was innovative at the time for having a fine metal mesh running through the soft silicone mould, which kept the edges of the little cakes crisp as they cooked. Madeleines were one of the first things I made for myself away from home, and always a riff on Mum's recipe. They are surprisingly quick and easy to make; the hardest part is waiting to bake them as the batter needs to rest for a few hours, but this means that they make the perfect dessert after an elaborate dinner, as they're delicious served straight from the oven, with a glass of something sweet and an espresso.

100g (1 stick minus 1 tbsp) unsalted butter, plus extra for greasing

a pinch of sea salt

1 tsp vanilla extract

¼ tsp finely grated unwaxed lemon zest

2 eggs

100g (½ cup plus 1 tbsp) caster (superfine) sugar

100g (¾ cup) plain (all-purpose) flour, plus extra for dusting

½ tsp baking powder

icing (confectioners') sugar, sifted, for dusting

Melt the butter with the salt, vanilla and lemon zest in a small pan over a medium heat, then leave to cool slightly.

In a mixing bowl, beat the eggs and caster sugar until pale and frothy. Gradually whisk in the lukewarm butter.

Sift the flour and baking powder into the bowl, then gently fold into the egg mixture to make a thick batter. Cover the bowl with a plate and leave to rest in the fridge for 2–4 hours, or overnight if you fancy – you should see some bubbles form on the top of the batter when it's sufficiently rested.

When ready to bake, heat the oven to 180°C fan (400°F/Gas 6). Grease and flour a madeleine tray – the batter makes about 12.

Spoon 1 tablespoon of the batter into each dip in the tray as they need space to rise. Bake for 10–12 minutes, until risen and golden. Dust with icing sugar and serve straight from the oven, if you like, or leave to cool on a wire rack.

Salted Honey Madeleines

¼ tsp sea salt

2 tbsp runny honey of choice

The type of honey you use really influences the flavour of these madeleines, while the sea salt balances the sweetness, reminding me of salted caramel. Stir both into the melted butter at the start of the recipe.

Marmalade Madeleines

3 tbsp marmalade

¼ tsp finely grated unwaxed orange zest

I like to use a bitter, thick-cut marmalade, but use whatever you best like to eat on toast and amplify it with a little grated fresh orange zest. Fold both through the batter just before you spoon it into the tray.

Marbled Madeleines

1 tbsp cocoa powder, sifted

For a little hint of chocolate, sift the cocoa powder into half of the batter. Spoon half plain batter and half chocolate batter into each dip in the tray, then swirl them together with the back of a table knife to give a marbled effect.

Comfort Crumble

A bowl of crumble can turn a day around. The meditative task of rubbing the cold cubes of butter into the sugar, flour and spices absorbs your attention, and is the wind-down I long for at the end of a busy day. On those rainy winter nights when you get home and the kitchen shelves look bare but you crave something that feels like pulling on a warm jumper (sweater), this is what to bake.

Use whatever fruit you can find, but I like the combination of apples or plums paired with tart berries as they form a sweet-and-sour compôte that cradles the spiced crumble topping. As the fruit bubbles up over the edges of the crumble as it bakes, they meld together to create something irresistible. Although I mostly make crumble for dessert, I do so because I want to eat the leftovers cold for breakfast the next morning.

FRUIT FILLING

400g (1lb) cooking apples (about 3 large), such as Bramley, peeled, cored and sliced, or plums, halved, stoned and quartered

150g (1 cup) blackberries, raspberries or gooseberries

1 tbsp soft light brown sugar

1 tbsp fresh root ginger, peeled and finely chopped

juice of ½ lemon

a pinch of ground cinnamon

CRUMBLE TOPPING

150g (heaped 1 cup) plain (all-purpose) flour

100g (½ cup) soft light brown sugar

50g (⅓ cup) whole rolled (old-fashioned) oats

3 tbsp flaked almonds or roughly chopped walnuts or hazelnuts

1 tsp ground ginger

1 tsp ground cinnamon

½ tsp ground cardamom

¼ tsp freshly grated nutmeg

a pinch of sea salt

100g (1 stick minus 1 tbsp) chilled salted butter, cubed

First make the filling. Add your choice of fruit to a 25 x 20cm (10 x 8in) baking dish with the berries, sugar, ginger, lemon juice and cinnamon. Stir until combined then let this sit and marinate while you make the crumble topping.

Meanwhile, heat the oven to 180°C fan (400°F/Gas 6).

To make the crumble topping, mix all the dry ingredients in a large mixing bowl, add the butter and rub it in with your fingertips to a crumbly consistency that looks like coarse damp sand.

Spoon the crumble mixture over the fruit to cover evenly and bake for 35–40 minutes. When it's ready, the crumble topping will be golden and the fruit bubbling up at the edges.

Serve with plenty of cold custard, a scoop or two of ice cream, or for breakfast I love it with a spoonful of thick Greek yogurt.

Aperitivo Hour

Cocktails start everything off right. I love the ceremony of making them and, for much of my adult life, my bar cart has been a source of inspiration, both in my cooking and as a special start to a meal. My friend, Ana, is famed for her regular Friday-night aperitivo hour, when each week she takes turns with her husband to choose a cocktail and pair it with snacks: an Americano with fennel salami and a sharp pecorino one week; and a French 75 with soft cheese and cornichons the next. I love the way that this ritual marks the end of the week and makes someone you love smile. Here are my favourite cocktails for two, each with a snack pairing.

Martini

I have a specific set of desires when it comes to how I like my martinis. Firstly, they need to be as cold as possible, so I freeze the martini mix for a few hours and make sure it's poured into an ice-cold glass. Secondly, wanting the best of both, I choose a twist *and* an olive. I'm a gin gal, but swap it for vodka, if you prefer.

200ml (scant 1 cup) gin

10ml (2 tsp) vermouth

1 unwaxed lemon

2 green olives

Mix the gin and vermouth, then freeze for a few hours until icy cold. Place 2 martini glasses in the freezer an hour before serving too. Pour the ice-cold martini mix into the chilled glasses.

Using a vegetable peeler, cut 2 long, thin pieces of lemon peel. Rub the peel over the rim of the glasses, then drop one into each glass. Place the olives on cocktail sticks, then balance atop each glass before serving.

SNACK

Caramelized mixed nuts, olives and shards of Parmesan cheese.

Negroni

There's nothing as good as a Negroni in a fancy bar before a night out. I like it classic – equal parts gin, Campari and vermouth – with a thin slice of frozen blood orange. When the blood orange season is coming to the end, I slice up a few and freeze them to use in cocktails throughout the year.

100ml (6½ tbsp) gin

100ml (6½ tbsp) Campari

100ml (6½ tbsp) red vermouth

ice

2 blood oranges, sliced into rounds and frozen

Pour the gin, Campari and vermouth into a glass, add ice to the top and stir. Finish with a frozen slice of blood orange (save the rest of the slices for use another day).

SNACK

Olive oil crisps, crostini topped with olive tapenade and slices of salami.

Margarita

Inspired by the incredible cocktail queen of London, Missy Flynn, and her addition of Campari to a margarita, this is all I want to drink at the end of a long week when it's still warm outside. If the lime juice is fresh and the tequila is strong, you can't go wrong.

100ml (6½ tbsp) tequila

25ml (1½ tbsp) Campari

½ tsp agave syrup/maple syrup/honey

70ml (5 tbsp) fresh lime juice

ice

slices of fresh lime and sea salt, to serve

Pour the tequila, Campari, agave syrup and lime juice into a cocktail shaker and shake, shake, shake. Pour into 2 glasses over ice and top each one with a slice of lime and a sprinkle of sea salt.

Bellini

A good bellini tastes like you're watching a sunset with someone you love. Originally created in Venice, it's worth waiting for white peach season to make these. I only purée one half of the peach, so you can still taste the pieces of fruit at the bottom of the glass after it's infused the wine.

1 white peach, peeled, stone removed and finely chopped

juice of ½ lemon

400ml (1¾ cup) sparkling white wine

Freeze the chopped white peach for a few hours until frozen. Blend half of the frozen peach with the lemon juice until smooth, then mix the purée with the remaining frozen peach pieces. Spoon the peach mix into the bottom of 2 glasses and top with sparkling white wine.

SNACK

Raw radishes dipped in sea salt and chilli flakes.

SNACK

Canned anchovies in oil, slices of baguette and butter curls.

The Best Banana Split

The pleasure of a sundae is that it's always better shared with someone you love; it's about the clinking of spoons fighting for the last bite of banana or the cherry covered with the most hot chocolate sauce. I am somewhat of a sundae specialist and have dedicated many hours to studying the structure of the best, and the one that I keep coming back to is the banana split. This is my version of the most perfect banana split: the maraschino cherries of the classic are replaced with fresh ripe red cherries; the bananas are carefully caramelized on one side, so they crack like the top of a crème brûlée when you sink your spoon in; and the hot chocolate sauce is dark with a hint of coffee. The whole lot is topped with salty-sweet flaked almonds. Serve at the table with a jug of extra sauce, which you'll undoubtedly want more of.

1 ripe (but not too ripe or bruised) banana, unpeeled

3 tbsp caster (superfine) sugar

50g (¾ cup) flaked almonds

2 pinches of sea salt

150g (1 cup) red cherries

90g (3¼oz) 70% plain (semisweet) chocolate, broken into pieces

120ml (½ cup) double (heavy) cream

a pinch of ground instant coffee

a tub of vanilla ice cream

Start by popping the banana into the freezer (this may seem odd, but there's method in my madness, I assure you) for 10–20 minutes while you carry on with the next steps.

Scatter 2 tablespoons of the sugar in a thin, even layer in a large, dry frying pan on a medium heat and warm for 2–3 minutes, until the sugar dissolves and turns an amber colour at the edges, but do not stir. Add the flaked almonds and give them a quick stir with a spatula to coat them in the caramelized sugar, then tip onto a baking (parchment) paper-lined plate. Sprinkle with a pinch of salt and let cool.

Using a small paring knife (or a cherry pitting tool, if you've got one), cut the cherries in half and remove the stones from most of them, leaving a few whole with the stems on to serve.

Melt the chocolate with the cream, a pinch of salt and the coffee in a double boiler, or in a heatproof bowl set over a pan of gently simmering water, stir until smooth. Set aside to cool a little.

Take the banana and the tub of vanilla ice cream out of the freezer to soften.

Peel the still-frozen banana and cut in half lengthways through the middle. Sprinkle the remaining sugar over the cut side of each banana half. Heat a dry frying pan on a medium-high heat. Add the banana halves to the pan, sugar-side down, and cook for 2 minutes, until the sugar turns golden and caramelizes. (The banana is cold enough not to cook, so only the sugar will caramelize.)

CHOCOLATE TRUFFLES

If you've got leftover sauce, you could turn it into truffles. Add ½ shot of dark rum, bourbon or amaretto to the sauce and pop the bowl in the fridge overnight to set firm. Scoop the set chocolate mixture into balls with a hot teaspoon, then roll each ball in cocoa powder to lightly dust all over.

To assemble, remove the banana halves from the pan and place in a serving dish with space in the centre for the ice cream. Top with 3 scoops of ice cream, a handful of cherries and a generous drizzle of the hot chocolate sauce, pouring the rest into a jug. Smash the almond brittle and scatter the pieces over the top. You're now ready to serve with 2 spoons. Bring the jug of extra sauce to the table for good measure.

Peach Melba

This classic dessert was originally created by Auguste Escoffier for the Australian opera singer, Dame Nellie Melba. At its heart, it is all about building a delicate balance between the sweet peaches, tart raspberries and mellow vanilla ice cream. Now, I have no issue with Escoffier, but what can't a little wine improve? I like to gently poach the peaches in wine until tender, then reduce the wine into a syrup with raspberries and a little lemon peel, which really intensifies the different elements of the dish. I prefer to use frozen raspberries as they crumble into little caviar-like jewels and add a burst of intense raspberry flavour to the peach and ice cream. You can prepare the different parts in advance, then assemble everything when you want to eat it.

200ml (scant 1 cup) dry white or rosé wine

½ tsp vanilla extract

1 tbsp caster (superfine) sugar

2 just-ripe peaches, halved and stones removed

100g (1 cup) frozen raspberries

strip of unwaxed lemon peel

1 tbsp light brown soft sugar

50g (scant ⅓ cup) macadamia nuts

a pinch of sea salt

a tub of vanilla ice cream

Pour the wine, vanilla and caster sugar into a large, heavy-bottomed pot over a medium-low heat and stir to combine. Add the peaches, cut-side down, and bring to a simmer. Turn the heat to low and simmer, with the lid on, for 15 minutes, until softened. Using a slotted spoon, remove the peaches from the wine, place them on a plate to cool, then chill until ready to serve. You can peel off the skins, if preferred, but you don't have to.

Add half of the raspberries to the wine mix with the lemon peel and turn the heat to high. Bring to the boil and cook for about 5 minutes, until the liquid has reduced by half and turned syrupy. Strain the syrup to remove any raspberry seeds and the lemon peel and leave to cool completely. Chill the syrup until ready to serve.

Meanwhile, make the caramelized nuts. Sprinkle the light brown soft sugar evenly over the base of a dry non-stick frying pan and turn the heat to high. Once the sugar starts to melt, add the macadamia nuts and tilt the pan to coat them in the caramel. Tip the caramelized nuts onto a baking (parchment) paper-lined baking tray, sprinkle with the sea salt and leave to cool and set. Break into pieces once set.

To assemble, place two halves of poached peach in each serving dish and top with a scoop of vanilla ice cream. Spoon the raspberry syrup over and top with the rest of the frozen raspberries and the caramelized macadamia.

Chocolate-Dipped Amaretti

When you're out of ideas and out of energy, this is the dessert to rescue you. I first made it years ago while cooking dinner for a pal, who I wanted to feed well and spoil, but had no time to make the dessert. The fun of eating it definitely outweighs anything that requires more time or ingredients – it simply involves going to your local deli, buying a box of the most beautifully wrapped amaretti you can find, a bar of plain (semisweet) chocolate and a pot of cream. This is all about the act of dipping something crunchy and sweet into a pool of melted bitter plain chocolate ganache. If you don't have, or can't find, amaretti, use whatever biscuits (cookies) you like; the most important thing here is the melted chocolate and the mess you'll most likely make sharing it.

a bag of crunchy (or soft) amaretti

50g (1¾oz) 70% plain (semisweet) chocolate, broken into pieces

100ml (6½ tbsp) double (heavy) cream

a pinch of sea salt

a splash of amaretto or your favourite liqueur, plus shots to serve (optional)

Tip the bag of amaretti into a large serving bowl.

Melt the chocolate in a double boiler with the cream, salt and amaretto, if using, then stir until combined and smooth. (You can also use a heatproof bowl set over a pan of gently simmering water.)

When the chocolate ganache is ready, bring the pot from the double boiler or the bowl to the table, or pour it into a serving bowl.

To serve, dunk the amaretti into the chocolate ganache with shots of amaretto and/or an espresso alongside, if you like.

Lemon and Lychee Sherbet
(with a shot)

Before I moved to London, I remember seeing photographs of parks here in the summer during a "heatwave", when the temperature was the same as a standard Sydney day: men with their shirts whipped off lounging in the fountains of Regent's Park; women laying out on towels in bikinis in Soho Square, and I couldn't imagine the city ever being that hot. That was until I lived through my first London heatwave when the pavement felt like it was melting my shoes and the rush of the tube past my cheek was the only breeze I'd felt for days. Every summer, I make sure to keep a container of this refreshing sherbet tucked away in the freezer for days like this.

Sherbet is a cross between an ice cream and a sorbet and is so simple to make. You don't need anything fancy, it's just a few ingredients blended together and frozen, but it looks and tastes spectacular. The vodka in the mix stops it freezing solid, while the cream gently mellows the intensity of the lemon and alcohol. The best part of this dessert is that it is an extraordinary vehicle for a shot of something. Inspired by my beloved St. John restaurant, where I always order their seasonal fruit sorbet with a shot of vodka (because who wants to decide between dessert and another drink?), I like either gin or tequila, here, which pair so perfectly with the perfumed aroma of the lychees. When you pour the shot over, the sherbet becomes reminiscent of a posh service station slushie. It's one of those desserts you want to have at the end of a rich meal, when you really truly don't have room for dessert but simply must have something sweet. Share it in the sunshine and soak up that feeling of summer.

600g (1lb 5oz) can lychees in syrup

juice of 1½ lemons

1–2 tbsp icing (confectioners') sugar (the quantity depends on how sweet your lemons and lychees are)

4 tsp double (heavy) cream

4 tsp vodka

a shot of gin, vodka or rum, to serve

Open the can of lychees and strain the syrup from the fruit over a bowl – you'll need about 200g (2 cups) fruit and 300ml (1¼ cups) lychee syrup. (Keep any leftover fruit or syrup for a martini.)

Put the lychees, syrup, lemon juice and the smaller quantity of sugar in a blender and blitz to a purée. Stir in the cream and vodka, then taste and add the rest of the sugar, if needed.

Pour the mixture into a freezer-proof container and freeze for about 4 hours, stirring every hour or so to break up the ice crystals, until frozen.

To serve, spoon the sherbet into balls with an ice-cream scoop that's been warmed first in hot water, or blitz briefly in a blender and serve like a granita - either way, serve piled high in glasses with a shot of something special on the side to pour over the top.

Part II

JUST TO DELIGHT

Just to Delight

Ironing a tablecloth; dusting off your candlesticks; buying a new set of napkins while googling "how to shuck an oyster"; and more bottles of wine than you'll need – the setting for an evening that you know will be treasured forever. This collection of recipes is for special times, putting to work the kitchen kit you perhaps only get out of the cupboard once or twice a year; and for those occasions that allow you to use up every inch of your dining table by filling it with plates, platters and flowers. It's for times when there is a dessert *and* a cheeseboard *and* a box of chocolates to graze on with a glass of something good. These are the recipes that you will return to once a year for birthdays and anniversaries. These are the pages that you will turn to for the nights you know you need to make magic; and for those moments that will be told and retold so many times to come.

Florence Buns

On our first holiday away together to Florence, with an early morning hangover after too many Negronis the night before, Joe and I practically crawled to the closest coffee shop for an espresso to ease our headaches. As Joe was getting the coffee, I went next door to the bakery for sustenance. It was early spring in the city and Easter was just around the corner, so the bakery was full of traditional Italian pastries, like *pastiera napoletana*, big boxes of *Colomba di Pasqua* and *pan di ramerino* or rosemary and raisin buns. I bought a few buns, then went to the supermarket next door for my failsafe hangover cure, orange juice, and picked up some sliced prosciutto too.

We took our bounty of snacks down to the edge of the Arno River and made a little picnic on the riverbank walls. I loved the marriage between the sweet raisins and earthy rosemary in the buns, especially when partnered with the salty prosciutto. My version of the buns is designed to be eaten with accompaniments like ham, cheese and tomatoes for a blended sweet/savoury breakfast. They're soft and fluffy on the inside and as soon as you tear them open, you can smell the aroma of rosemary and raisins.

175ml (¾ cup) lukewarm water

8g (scant 2 tsp) instant dried yeast

1 tbsp runny honey

1 tsp caster (superfine) sugar

1 tbsp olive oil

250g (1¾ cups) strong white bread flour, plus extra for dusting

½ tsp sea salt

2 tsp finely chopped fresh rosemary

3 tbsp roughly chopped seedless raisins

1 tbsp salted butter, melted, plus extra for greasing

fennel salami, prosciutto or mortadella, cheese and sliced tomato, to serve

---

Pour the lukewarm water into a bowl and whisk in the yeast, honey, sugar and olive oil until combined, then leave for a few minutes until the water starts to foam a little.

Mix the flour and salt in a separate mixing bowl until the salt is evenly distributed, then make a well in the middle. Pour the water and yeast mixture into the well and stir until combined.

Tip the dough out on a lightly floured work surface and knead for 10 minutes. It will be a little wet and sticky to start with, but will become smooth and elastic by the end and should come away from your hands with no resistance. In the last few minutes of kneading, add the rosemary and raisins and shape the dough into a ball.

Place the dough in a lightly greased bowl, cover and leave to rise in a warm place for 2 hours, until doubled in size.

Punch the risen dough to knock back, then shape into a ball. Using a sharp knife, cut the dough into 8 equal pieces. Roll each piece into a round bun and place on a baking (parchment) paper-lined baking tray, spaced apart to allow them room to rise. Cover loosely and leave to prove for 1 hour, taking care not to knock out any of the air as they rise.

Heat the oven to 200°C fan (425°F/Gas 7).

Bake the buns for 18–20 minutes, until golden brown on top. As soon as the rolls come out of the oven, brush the tops with the melted butter. I love them filled with sharp fennel salami, prosciutto or mortadella, cheese and sliced tomato.

Breakfast Buckle Cake

Sometimes a slice of cake for breakfast is a sure-fire start to a good day. This cake is inspired by the American buckle cake – the weight of the fruit placed on top sinks or "buckles" beneath the cake batter as it bakes, hence the name. I love making this cake in summer when my fruit bowl is at its most abundant. The cake is not too sweet making it ideal for the morning, and it's almost cheesecake-like texture, thanks to the ricotta, cuts through the sweetness of whatever fruit you choose to use. I love to top it with strawberries, since when baked they create an almost jammy layer to sink your spoon into.

80g (5 tbsp) salted butter, softened, plus extra for greasing

100g (½ cup plus 1 tbsp) caster (superfine) sugar

1 egg, lightly beaten

175ml (¾ cup) buttermilk

100g (½ cup minus 2 tsp) ricotta cheese

1 tsp vanilla extract

1 tsp finely grated unwaxed lemon, orange, grapefruit or lime zest

a pinch of ground nutmeg

130g (1 cup) plain (all-purpose) flour, plus extra for dusting

½ tsp bicarbonate of soda (baking soda)

½ tsp baking powder

150g (5½oz) strawberries, halved or quartered if large, plus extra to serve

1 tbsp icing (confectioners') sugar (optional)

Greek yogurt, to serve

Heat the oven to 180°C fan (400°F/Gas 6). Line the base of a 15cm (6in) square cake tin with baking (parchment) paper and butter and flour the sides.

In a large mixing bowl, cream the butter and sugar using an electric hand whisk until fluffy and pale in colour. Add the egg, buttermilk, ricotta, vanilla, citrus zest of choice and nutmeg and whisk until smooth.

Sift together the flour, bicarbonate of soda and baking powder in a separate mixing bowl, then fold in thirds into the ricotta mix until combined.

Spoon the cake batter into the lined tin and level the top with a palette knife. Gently place the strawberries on top of the cake and bake for 50 minutes, until risen and golden, and the strawberries have caramelized in places.

Leave the cake to cool completely in the tin, then turn out onto a serving plate and dust the top with icing sugar, if you like. Serve with extra strawberries and Greek yogurt.

OTHER FRUIT OPTIONS

- *Mango, cut into bite-sized pieces, and lime zest*

- *Apricots, stoned and quartered, and almond extract instead of citrus zest*

- *Green apple, peeled and cut into thin moons, and lemon zest*

- *Figs, quartered, and citrus zest*

- *Pear, peeled and cut into bite-sized pieces, with chunks of dark chocolate folded through the batter.*

Spiced Rice Pudding and Gingery Rhubarb

Most of my favourite comfort foods come from early childhood. They're the dishes I grew up eating and are so intertwined with my memories of being a kid that I can hardly remember when I first tasted them. That said, one of my ultimate comfort foods, to both eat and cook, comes from my tempestuous teenage years: rice pudding wasn't a dish that my mum made for us as children, and growing up in Singapore the closest thing I ate was probably congee.

Now, as I write, there is no one in the world that I would rather spend an afternoon eating with than Mum, but during my drama-queen teenage years, I took everything out on her. When I got home from school each day, exhausted from school-yard bullies, homework and the complexities of being a teenager, I just wanted to disappear into an album and go to sleep. It was around this time, Mum started to make me rice pudding; on getting home, I would smell the rice, milk and spices gently simmering on the stove. I think because rice pudding was new to me, it sparked my interest and, wanting to find out how it was made, I'd start to come into the kitchen and stir the pot, while Sydney's winter rain battered against the kitchen windows. By the time the pudding was poured into little bowls, we'd spent an afternoon talking and we haven't really stopped since.

In an interview a few years ago, I was asked my top five comfort foods and without skipping a beat the first thing that came to mind was Mum's rice pudding. This version is spiced with aromatics like cinnamon, cardamom and bay and uses arborio rice, normally reserved for risotto. The spice mix brings a gentle warmth and the arborio adds a smooth, velvety texture to the pudding that pairs so well with the tartness of the roasted rhubarb.

SPICED RICE PUDDING

170g (scant 1 cup) arborio rice

1 litre (4½ cups) whole milk

1 bay leaf

½ star anise

1 cinnamon stick

1 long strip of unwaxed lemon peel

1 clove

2 cardamom pods, split

a pinch of sea salt

60g (⅓ cup) caster (superfine) sugar

1 tsp vanilla extract

¼ tsp ground nutmeg

100ml (6½ tbsp) single (light) cream

1 tbsp Greek yogurt

GINGERY RHUBARB

juice of 1 large orange, preferably blood orange

2 tsp caster (superfine) sugar

¼ tsp finely grated fresh root ginger

2 rhubarb stalks, chopped into 5cm long pieces

Into a large, heavy-bottomed pot, add the rice and milk along with the bay leaf, star anise, cinnamon stick, lemon peel, clove, cardamom, salt and sugar. Give everything a good stir and bring to a gentle simmer over a medium heat.

Once simmering, turn the heat down to low and gently stir so the rice doesn't stick to the bottom. It looks like a lot of milk but trust the process and it will be perfect. Let the pudding simmer on low for 25 minutes, stirring every few minutes, or until each grain is soft but still has a bit of bite. Once it's done, turn the heat off.

Stir in the vanilla and nutmeg and pour the rice pudding into a large serving bowl or container. As you're doing this, take out the whole spices. Press a sheet of baking (parchment) paper on the surface of the rice pudding and leave to cool. When cool, pop

the pudding in the fridge to chill for at least 4 hours and let the rice absorb the spiced milk. Stir in the cream and yogurt before serving to give it a gorgeously custardy consistency and extra richness.

You can either make the gingery rhubarb ahead of time if you want to serve it cold and syrupy, or just before serving, if you'd like it warm. Heat the oven to 180°C fan (400°F/Gas 6). In a small bowl, mix the orange juice, sugar and ginger until the sugar dissolves. Put the rhubarb in a small, deep baking dish and pour the orange juice mix over. Roast the rhubarb for 15 minutes, until tender but it still holds its shape.

Serve the warm rhubarb and any juices spooned over the cold rice pudding or pop it in the fridge to chill, so the rhubarb turns gorgeous and sticky, until ready to serve.

Just to Delight

Pancakes

Pancakes are perfect because they make you pause: between the building of the batter; the bubbling of the butter in the pan; and waiting for the curling edges of the pancakes as they cook, they make you stand and stop. They are the best breakfast to give you some time to think about whatever happened the night before, or whatever you'd like the coming day to bring; the antithesis of a bowl of cereal eaten over the sink. Between the flip of each pancake, there is time to talk and do other things – make coffee, slice oranges, set the table.

They were the first thing I ever learnt to cook, standing on a chair stirring the batter an arm's length away from Mum. Pancakes have made a lifetime of mornings seem magical, from schoolgirl sleepovers to first-friendship hangovers, and new lovers lingering the morning after. And still today they are the first thing I make for anyone I love in my life. The seemingly bland ingredients blend into a beige bliss, created from everyday ingredients that are often overlooked.

To make my version of the best breakfast for two, I use buttermilk in the batter. It's an instant texture and flavour changer; the difference between eating a slice of plain white bread and a good sourdough. This recipe makes more than enough small, thick pancakes for two with leftovers. Since pancakes are personal, there is a choice of toppings and a savoury option, too, depending on what you fancy.

200g (1½ cups) plain (all-purpose) flour

½ tsp baking powder

½ tsp bicarbonate of soda (baking soda)

200ml (scant 1 cup) buttermilk

100ml (6½ tbsp) whole milk

1 egg

2 tsp caster (superfine) sugar

a pinch of sea salt

45g (3 tbsp) unsalted butter

Sift the flour, baking powder and bicarbonate of soda into a large mixing bowl and mix together, then make a well in the middle.

In a separate bowl, whisk the buttermilk, milk, egg, caster sugar and salt. Pour this into the well in the dry ingredients and stir to combine – don't overmix, it doesn't matter about a few lumps and bumps. Leave the batter to rest for 15 minutes while you sort out coffee and what you're going to have on top of your pancakes.

When you're ready to start cooking the pancakes, melt half of the butter in a large non-stick frying pan and stir it into the batter; it should feel like pushing a spoon through thick custard when combined.

Heat the pan again on a medium heat, adding a little more of the butter. Spoon in a small ladleful of the batter per pancake and cook for about 2 minutes, wait until bubbles appear on the surface and the bottom of the pancake is golden before you turn it, then cook the other side for another minute. Transfer the pancake to a plate – the first will never be the best, but it can be the cook's perk.

Continue to cook the pancakes (it makes about 10–12), adding more butter when needed. Keep them warm in a low oven if you want to serve them in a stack, or plate them up one at a time if you really can't wait. Serve with your choice of filling or topping – see opposite for ideas. I like to eat any leftover pancakes cold with butter and jam.

Toppings and Fillings

Citrus and Sugar

a mix of oranges, lemons and grapefruits

a small bowl of caster (superfine) sugar

Over a large bowl, peel away the citrus skin and segment the fruit. Using a small sharp knife, cut between the membranes to remove a perfect little moon-shaped fruit slice. Do this over a bowl, so you don't lose any juice and squeeze any leftover pith from the fruit into the bowl. Bring the bowl of segmented fruit and juice to the table alongside a little bowl of sugar. Top the pancakes with a little citrus fruit and a sprinkling of sugar.

Blueberry and Cardamom Compôte

200g (1½ cups) blueberries (fresh or frozen)

100ml (6½ tbsp) maple syrup

a pinch of ground cardamom

a pinch of ground cinnamon

juice of ½ lemon

Into a small pan, add the blueberries and pour the maple syrup over. Turn the heat to low and let the berries simmer for about 10 minutes, until they start to burst. Stir in the cardamom and cinnamon and take the pan off the heat once the blueberry mix becomes a brilliant deep-purple sauce. Squeeze in the lemon juice and mix before spooning over your pancakes.

Cheddar and Chive Pancakes

50g (½ cup) coarsely grated mature Cheddar cheese

3 tbsp chopped chives

a pinch of ground nutmeg

plenty of freshly ground black pepper

¼ tsp English mustard powder

Make the pancake batter following the instructions left and let it rest.

Just before you want to start cooking the pancakes, stir the Cheddar, chives, nutmeg, pepper and mustard powder into the batter. Cook in the same way as instructed in the pancake recipe, left – as the cheese melts it will create the most sublime crisp edges.

Serve the pancakes with bacon and avocado, or with smoked salmon and a squeeze of lemon.

Spinach, Cheese and Herb Pie

The combination of green leafy spinach, salty crumbly feta and lots of fresh herbs encased in a filo (phyllo) pastry crust is exactly what I want to eat for breakfast when cereal and toast just won't do. You can serve a slice of the pie solo, but I love it with a fried egg and a simple tomato salad on the side. It's the sort of thing I like to make early morning for breakfast on a long weekend, then snack on slices throughout the day; your kitchen may be covered in filo crumbs, but it's worth it. You could, of course, get creative and roll it into a swirl, like the traditional *börek*, but this flat-topped version means that the fennel and sesame seeds sprinkled over at the end become gloriously golden during baking.

200g (7oz) feta cheese, roughly chopped

250g (1 cup plus 1 tbsp) ricotta cheese

160g frozen leaf spinach, defrosted and squeezed dry

1½ tsp finely grated unwaxed lemon zest

1 handful of finely chopped mint

1 handful of finely chopped dill

1 handful of finely chopped flat-leaf parsley

1 tsp sea salt, plus extra to finish

½ tsp freshly ground black pepper

2 garlic cloves, finely grated

1½ tsp fennel seeds

270g (9½oz) filo (phyllo) pastry, 6 sheets in total

100ml (6½ tbsp) olive oil, plus extra for greasing

1 tsp sesame seeds

Heat the oven to 200°C fan (425°F/Gas 7). Line the base of a 28 x 22cm (11 x 8½in), and 5cm/2in deep, baking tin with baking (parchment) paper and lightly brush the sides with olive oil.

Mix the feta, ricotta, spinach, lemon zest, herbs, salt, pepper, garlic and ½ teaspoon of the fennel seeds in a large mixing bowl with either a wooden spoon or an electric hand whisk until smooth.

Separate the sheets of filo pastry and cover 3 of the sheets with a damp tea towel to prevent them drying out, and set aside. Lay the other half down on a chopping board. Place a sheet of filo in the oiled, lined baking tin and repeat until 3 sheets of filo are layered on top of one another, brushing each layer with a little more oil. The excess pastry may come over the sides of the tin, but that's fine and don't worry if it looks messy at this stage as it will be sorted soon.

Spoon the spinach and cheese mix over the the filo base, then spread it out in an even layer. Place a sheet of filo from the reserved 3 sheets over the top of the filling, firmly pressing it flat and tucking in the edges to seal in the filling. Brush over more olive oil and repeat the layering process until you've used all the filo sheets, then tuck any overhang down the sides of the tin.

Brush the top with more olive oil. Scatter the rest of the fennel seeds and the sesame seeds with a pinch of salt over the top of the pastry and bake for 35 minutes, until golden brown. Serve cut into slices, warm or at room temperature.

Latkes With Smoked Salmon and Dill

The epitome of good-mood food for me is latkes. I love the task of grating the potatoes and squishing out all the water before frying them. Latkes feel like special occasion, celebration food, and I like to make a platter of these canape-sized potato cakes just for the two of us whenever a moment needs to be marked. When we first moved into Oslo Court, I went to our local Jewish deli, Panzer's, for smoked salmon and soured cream to serve with latkes and to celebrate unpacking the kitchen boxes. We sipped champagne on the balcony, ignored the rest of the boxes we had to unpack and ate a platter of crisp hot latkes topped with cold soured cream, curls of smoked salmon and plenty of torn dill. I use 2 forks to scoop up the potato mixture, which creates the most gorgeous lace-like edge to each latke, so they get as crunchy as can be.

500g (1lb 2oz) potatoes, such as Maris Piper, about 2–3 in total, peeled and coarsely grated

½ tsp sea salt

1 egg white

3 tsp cornflour (cornstarch)

plenty of freshly ground black pepper, plus extra to finish

1 tbsp salted butter

3 tbsp flavourless oil, such as sunflower

120ml (scant 1 cup) soured cream

100g (3½oz) smoked salmon

plenty of fresh dill, chopped

1 lemon, cut into wedges

Heat the oven to a 160°C fan (350°F/Gas 4).

Place the grated potato in the middle of a clean tea towel and evenly sprinkle the salt over. Let the potato sit for a few minutes, then gather up the sides of the tea towel and twist the top to make a bundle. Squeeze like mad to extract as much water from the potato as possible. When you think there is nothing left to squeeze, let it sit for a minute, then squeeze one last time.

In a large mixing bowl, whisk the egg white, 2 teaspoons of the cornflour and a good grinding of black pepper until foamy. Stir in the potato until the egg white mixture coats each strand. Use 2 forks to fluff the mixture up slightly.

Heat the butter and oil in a large non-stick frying pan on a medium-high heat. When the oil is hot and you're just about ready to fry, sprinkle the remaining cornflour over the potato, mix and fluff it up again with a fork until combined. Test the oil is hot enough with a strand of potato: if it starts to sizzle, it's ready.

Use 2 forks to lift walnut-sized amounts of the potato mix into the pan and fry for 4 minutes, on each side, until golden brown. Cook the latkes in batches of 3–4, so you don't overcrowd the pan; you should get about 12–15 in total.

Line a baking tray with a few sheets of kitchen paper. Place the cooked latkes on the lined tray to absorb any excess oil and keep warm in a low oven. Arrange the latkes on a large serving plate and top each one with a spoonful of soured cream, the smoked salmon, lots of chopped dill and plenty of black pepper. Serve with wedges of lemon for squeezing over.

Boxty With Butter-Fried Eggs

During my first 8 years in London, the cafe I went to for refuge, on days when all I wanted was food that tasted like someone special had cooked for me, was J&A Cafe in Clerkenwell. Just around the corner from my flat, it was an Irish cafe where the menu felt like home. The tea was always Barry's and the chutney Ballymaloe, it was a sanctuary that smelt like freshly baked bread and butter.

J&A opened in 2008 and closed in 2020, and the sadness I feel still when I walk past and can't pop in for an all-day breakfast is immense. What I've missed most is their boxty. These potato cakes are absolute heaven for breakfast. A slight deviation from the classic, more pancake-like boxty, these are inspired by the J&A ones that were like a mix of Irish champ (mashed potatoes with spring/green onions) and what my grandmother would call a rissole. On the J&A menu, above the boxty, they had a traditional rhyme these cakes inspired, "*Boxty on the griddle, boxty on the pan; if you can't make boxty, you'll never get a man*," which used to make me laugh. Sing the rhyme to whoever you make the boxty for, while they watch so they can make them for you next time, while you sleep in, read a book and wait for breakfast in bed.

BOXTY

3 starchy white potatoes, about 500g (1lb 2oz) in total, peeled and quartered

30g (2 tbsp) salted butter

6 spring (green) onions or wild garlic leaves (ramsons) when in season, finely chopped

¼ tsp freshly grated nutmeg

1 heaped tbsp plain (all-purpose) flour

sea salt and freshly ground black pepper

tomato chutney (preferably Ballymaloe), to serve

BUTTER-FRIED EGGS

30g (2 tbsp) salted butter

4 eggs

Boil the potatoes in a big pot of salted water until tender enough to pierce with a knife (this should take about 10–15 minutes or so).

As the potatoes cook, heat half the butter in a small frying pan, add the spring onions and sauté for 3 minutes, until tender. Take the pan off the heat, add the nutmeg and season with salt and pepper.

When the potatoes are ready, drain well, then return them to the hot pan to steam dry in the heat. Mash using your preferred device – I like to use a potato ricer. Once smooth, mix in the spring onions with a wooden spoon until they are evenly distributed. Sprinkle over the flour and mix well to combine. Using damp hands, form the mash into 2 large potato cakes and place on a lightly greased plate to chill for at least 2 hours (1 hour in the freezer), or preferably overnight.

When you're ready to cook the potato cakes, turn the oven to 150°C fan (340°F/Gas 3). Lightly dust the cakes in a hanful of flour, evenly coating the outside before frying.

Melt the remaining butter in a large frying pan and fry the potato cakes for 5 minutes, on each side, until crisp and golden.

Put the boxty on a lined baking tray in the oven for about 10 minutes while you fry the eggs. On a medium-high heat, melt the butter in the same pan that you fried the boxty in and let it start to sizzle and foam. Crack in the eggs and fry, using a spatula to distribute the butter around the edges so they get lovely and crisp. Season the eggs with salt and pepper and serve with the boxty and plenty of tomato chutney on the side.

The Romance of Food

Like many teenagers and early twenty-somethings, I felt lost for a long time at that age, never quite knowing what I wanted to do with my life. I always vaguely knew that I wanted to write, but for a while it felt beyond reach. There were two days in law school, a brief flirtation with wanting to be a filmmaker and then the year I spent working on a magazine for barristers (the ones in wigs, not the ones that make coffee). I was a nanny throughout university looking after nine-month-old twin boys, three gorgeous girls and two teenagers (not all at the same time) in Primrose Hill, London. I spent 6 months at the restaurant, St. John, as an "office assistant", where I didn't do much assisting, but I did do a lot of eating and, even then, I didn't think that working in food was for me.

Food and cooking were always my solace outside of work; they were what I'd wrap myself up in at the weekend as I ignored university essays and what I turned to when I wanted to feel like myself. There was a moment though, towards the end of my early twenties, while unpacking groceries after a trip to my local Turkish grocer, when it hit me that this was when I felt happiest. Of course, I was too terrified to do anything about it and spent years stashing away recipes written on the back of napkins. I often spent lunch breaks in cafes hiding away from colleagues at the advertising agency/ lingerie brand/department store I worked at as a part-time copywriter, so I could start freelancing for magazines. I kept thinking back to how I felt unpacking that shopping bag full of quince, huge bouquets of parsley, brick-sized blocks of feta and soft, white, sesame-sprinkled simit.

From the age of three to 13 I lived in Singapore, around the corner from one of the city's best wet markets and next to a hawker centre that we'd go to on Friday nights for fresh watermelon juice, roti *prata*, *bee hoon* noodles and Hainanese chicken rice. The produce in Singapore was – and still is – second to none: rambutans that looked like pom-poms and tasted like candy; mangosteens that stained my fingers as I scooped the pale-white fruit out of the

purple shell; and durian, of course, coined the "king of fruits", stacked high outside supermarkets. I was enamoured with everything in those markets, especially the fresh produce.

When we moved back to Australia when I was a teenager, it was the first time I had lived outside of Singapore's single season of hot and humid. The biggest difference between fresh produce in Singapore and that of Australia at the time was that most in Australia was locally grown: from the Queensland mangoes we'd buy in boxes on the side of the road at Christmas and golf-ball-sized white cherries to the tomatoes Granny grew in her garden, and the highly prized persimmons and loquats that would inspire awe at the Italian deli.

When I eventually found myself working as a food writer, I got the chance to go on trips to Greece to interview cheesemakers, to Spain to spend time with the black-hoofed pigs that become *jamón ibérico*, and to Ireland to meet a man who distilled whiskey in the shadow of Slane Castle. I loved every minute of it, but the people I loved to visit most were the fruit and vegetable growers.

For me, fruit and vegetables are inherently romantic. It seems like magic that a small seed can grow into a piece of fruit, or a field of vegetables that starts almost from nothing could become a three-course menu. To see the land shift with the seasons and transform from barren to lush and green requires dedication and faith on the part of the grower. On a visit to an organic farm just outside Tokyo, with Mount Fuji in the distance, I pulled a radish bigger than my arm out of the earth – I swear my heart skipped a beat.

Now, the thrill of going to the farmers' market to buy fruit and vegetables is the highlight of my week. I swoon at the sight of a watermelon or the perfume of a perfectly ripe peach, and count down to the first apricot, tomato or strawberry of the summer. Cooking seasonally is all I know how to do. Get excited about the produce you cook with, for each fresh ingredient is the beginning of something beautiful.

Stars of the Seasons

(a rough guide to the fresh produce I get most excited about cooking with)

Early Spring

Wild Garlic, Purple Sprouting Broccoli, New Potatoes, Collard Greens, Spring Onions, Fennel

Late Spring

Indian Mangoes, Loquats, Artichokes, Asparagus, Peas, Radishes, Watercress, Samphire.

Early Summer

Strawberries, Raspberries, Elderflower, Apricots, Summer Squash, Courgettes (Zucchini).

Late Summer

Peaches, Plums, Nectarines, Cherries, Corn, Tomatoes, Melons, Aubergines (Eggplants), Blueberries, Gooseberries.

Early Autumn

Figs, Swiss Chard, Damsons, Celeriac, Cauliflower, Elderberries, Runner Beans, Turnips.

Late Autumn

Pumpkins, Apples, Chestnuts, Chicory, Cranberries, Wild Mushrooms, Swedes (Rutabegas).

Early Winter

Brussels Sprouts, Kumquats, Lemons, Oranges, Pomegranates, Clementines, Mandarins, Quince.

Late Winter

Radicchio, Blood Oranges, Forced Rhubarb, Cime di Rapa, Puntarelle, Grapefruit, Kohlrabi, Persimmons.

Grilled Seafood With Green Sauce

I've been away for over 10 years now but when I go back home to Australia, I always follow the same ritual: after the 24-hour flight from London and the unfurling of limbs, all I want to see is the ocean, and experience the salty sea air filling my London lungs, and hold my cat Ming.

Of all the meals I've cooked, there is one I'll never forget – a table set for two, one plate for me and one for Ming. She has been my "baby" since I was 10 when she was given to me by my Mum as a three-week-old kitten that she'd found inside a plastic bag at the wet market in Singapore. Through my rough teenage years, her fur was constantly damp with tears; she's been there through it all and knows everything.

We've shared a lot, but most of all, we share an appetite. She's from a long line of street-market cats and would happily climb up a tablecloth to get to a roast chicken or shred paper bags to chew the corners off a fresh baguette. We share pancakes and spaghetti, and every Christmas she has her own plate of ham, turkey and stuffing.

Years ago, upon returning home, I knew I had to make Ming something special to make up for my time away. She sat on top of the kitchen bench watching me while I tossed prawns (shrimp) in chopped red chilli, garlic, lemon zest and olive oil, then grilled them until charred. Once done, I squeezed over more lemon and put them on a plate. With Ming sitting next to me, I ate each prawn, one by one, with a sip of very chilled white wine between each bite. Ming crunched her way through the shells, prawn heads and tails. She loved the chilli, she loved the garlic, and all that was left afterwards was an empty wine glass and two ladies lounging. Both neither as young, nor as foolish, as when we first came into each other's lives but still sharing the same appetite.

---

6 large raw prawns (shrimp), the biggest you can get your hands on

6 prepared scallops in the half shell

150g (1¼ sticks) salted butter, melted

4 garlic cloves, finely grated

1 small bunch of parsley, leaves finely chopped

finely grated zest and juice of 1 unwaxed lemon

1 tbsp capers, drained and finely chopped

1 large red chilli (chile), finely chopped

½ tsp sea salt

plenty of freshly ground black pepper

lemon wedges and bread, to serve

Heat the grill or barbecue to high.

Using a heavy, sharp knife, cut the prawns (shrimp) lengthways down the middle of the body, from the tail end to the head. You don't want to cut them all the way through, just enough to split them in half. I like to keep the heads and tails on too, but that's up to you; just don't forget to remove the black vein that runs down the middle. Lay the prawns and scallops in their shells on a baking tray.

Mix the melted butter with the garlic, most of the parsley, the lemon zest and juice, capers, chilli, salt and pepper. Spoon the butter mix over the prawns and scallops.

Place the prawns on the rack under the grill and cook for 5–6 minutes, turning halfway. Add the scallops to the grill after 3 minutes and cook until just opaque.

Season with extra salt and pepper and serve with wedges of lemon for squeezing over, the remaining parsley and a really good loaf of bread.

Crab, Fennel and Saffron Capellini

On a menu, I would order crab over lobster every time and this plate of pasta is my idea of a perfect dish. Crab is so tender and sweet it doesn't need much to make it stand out in a dish and I could happily eat it with nothing else on a piece of toast. When fresh crab has been out of my budget, I've also made this pasta with canned crab, and it works just as well. If you can find Pastis it really enhances the deep aniseed flavour of the fennel, and you'll find yourself reaching for it whenever you cook seafood. You can use any sort of long, thin pasta, which pairs so nicely with the delicate crab and saffron.

250g (9oz) long, thin dried pasta, such as capellini (angel hair)

30g (2 tbsp) salted butter

1 fennel bulb, cored and thinly sliced (save the fennel fronds for finishing the dish)

a splash of Pastis or dry white wine

3 garlic cloves, finely chopped

a big pinch of saffron strands, steeped in 2 tsp warm water

200g (7oz) white crab meat

finely grated zest and juice of 1 unwaxed lemon

4 tsp olive oil

a pinch of dried chilli (crushed red pepper) flakes

2 tbsp finely chopped parsley leaves

sea salt and freshly ground black pepper

Cook the pasta in a big pot of boiling salted water following the packet instructions.

While the pasta is cooking, melt 1 tablespoon of the butter in a large sauté pan on a medium-high heat. Add the fennel and sauté for 5 minutes, until softened and just starting to colour. Pour in the Pastis or wine to deglaze the pan and stir well. Add the garlic and saffron with its soaking water, then stir until everything turns a deep golden yellow.

Next, add the crab, lemon zest and juice, olive oil and chilli, stir gently to combine, so you don't break up the crab meat too much, and heat through for about a minute. Turn the heat off, taste and season with plenty of salt and pepper.

When the pasta is ready, use tongs to scoop it out of the cooking water into the pan of crab and fennel. Stir in the remaining butter, the parsley and a little of the pasta cooking water to loosen, and toss to combine. Serve in bowls with the fennel fronds scattered over the top.

Saltwater
and Sunshine

**This is a meal you want to eat with a breeze on your cheeks
and blue skies above you. Get messy and fight over the fish
cheeks, feta and the last roast potato.**

**Tomato Salad With Garlic and Almond Dressing •
Whole Roasted Fish With Lemon and Bay • Crispy Potatoes
With Oregano, Olives and Feta • Cherry and Apricot Tart**

A year or so ago, I spent my birthday alone in
the mountains of Andalusia, Spain. I was away
for a week on a writing retreat in a rural part
of the region and spent 12-hours a day sitting in
silence. It was my first time leaving the UK after
almost 18 months of on-and-off-again lockdowns.
On the morning of my birthday, even though I
was among the staggering beauty of the rugged
mountains, blue skies and fruit trees, I felt bereft
to be away from home and craved something
familiar. I packed a bag and called a local taxi
to drive me through the winding mountains as
the only thing I really wanted for my birthday
was to swim in the sea.

   The driver dropped me off and said she'd
be back at the same spot in a few hour's time.
I walked down to the bright white sand and saw
a near-empty beach. That swim was the first time

the sea had touched my skin since I'd left Sydney
almost two years before. With my hair still a little
wet and salty, I took myself out for lunch and ate
a meal that I've tried to recreate many times since
for the people I wish I'd shared it with that first
time: a simple tomato salad, a cold *ajoblanco*,
and roasted fish and crispy potatoes. This menu
captures the essence of that lunch.

   I like any meal that makes you slow down,
and nothing quite does that like sharing a whole
fish, which requires you to take time over. It's a
good idea to make the salad dressing and fruit tart
and par-boil your potatoes ahead of time so you have
less to do just before serving. This is the sort of meal
that I like to share sitting outside in a garden on
a hot day; it's definitely holiday-sort-of-food that
you want to rinse your hands in the sea after eating,
and sleep off in the late afternoon sun.

Tomato Salad With Garlic and Almond Dressing

This sliced tomato salad is paired with a dressing inspired by the cold Spanish soup, *ajoblanco*. The combination of the almonds, bread and garlic makes a cross between a dressing and a dip. Tomato and tarragon is one of my favourite pairings, and I love the torn leaves of the herb loosely scattered over the top.

3–4 large ripe heirloom tomatoes, cut into 1cm (½in) thick slices
1 small bunch of tarragon, leaves roughly torn
1 small bunch of mint, leaves roughly torn
½ red onion, thinly sliced
plenty of freshly ground black pepper

DRESSING

1 slice of white bread, crusts removed
150ml (⅔ cup) whole milk
40g (⅓ cup) whole blanched almonds
2 garlic cloves, peeled and left whole
6 tbsp extra-virgin olive oil, plus extra to serve
½ tsp sea salt, plus extra to season
1½ tbsp red/white wine vinegar or sherry vinegar

Start by making the dressing. Put the slice of bread in a shallow bowl, pour the milk over and leave to soak for 5 minutes.

While the bread is soaking, toast the almonds in a large, dry frying pan until they start to catch some colour and turn a little golden. While still warm, tip the almonds into a blender with the garlic, olive oil, salt, vinegar, the soaked bread and any remaining milk in the bowl. Blend until smooth and pour onto a serving platter.

Lay the tomatoes on top of the roasted almond dressing with the slices slightly overlapping. Scatter over the fresh herbs and red onion and drizzle with extra olive oil. Season with salt and plenty of black pepper.

Whole Roasted Fish With Lemon and Bay

The flavour you get when cooking a fish whole on the bone is unlike anything else. The fish is tender and sweet and looks so impressive presented on a platter. Use whatever whole white fish you fancy – a red mullet, snapper or sea bass are what I usually go for depending on what the fishmonger has on offer. The fish can roast in the oven at the same time as the potatoes, so everything is ready together.

3 garlic cloves, peeled and left whole

1 big handful of parsley, leaves and stalks

2 tbsp olive oil

1 tsp sea salt

2 unwaxed lemons, 1 juiced and 1 finely sliced

600–800g (1lb 5oz–1¾lb) whole white fish of your choice, gutted, descaled and cleaned

3 bay leaves

30cm (12in) piece of kitchen twine

Heat the oven to 180°C fan (400°F/Gas 6). (Put the potatatoes in the oven 15 minutes before the fish.) Using a pestle and mortar or blender, grind or blend the garlic with the parsley, olive oil, salt and the juice of 1 lemon into a paste.

With a very sharp knife, make 3–4 slits on each side of the fish. Line a large baking tray with a sheet of baking (parchment) paper that is double its size.

Place the fish in the middle of the lined tray and spoon the garlic and parsley paste over both sides of the fish, rubbing it into the cuts, then stuff the cavity with the sliced lemon, bay leaves and a sprinkle of salt.

Fold the sides of the paper over to encase the fish, then tie the twine around the middle to secure the paper, so it looks a bit like a present.

Roast the fish for 30 minutes, then take a peek in the parcel - it is cooked when the flesh readily flakes away from the bone. Lift the fish out of the parcel onto a serving dish, spoon over any juices, and serve with the tomato salad and crispy potatoes.

Crispy Potatoes With Oregano, Olives and Feta

There is nothing more irresistible to me than the combination of hot and cold in the same dish; I love warm chocolate sauce spooned over a scoop of cold vanilla ice cream in a sundae, or hot chips dipped in cold tartare sauce eaten on the beach. These potatoes are just as good with their hot crisp coating of semolina and topping of cold crumbled feta and green olives. Put them in the oven about 15 minutes before the fish, then they will both be ready at the same time. To get ahead, par-boil the potatoes and leave them to cool in advance.

1kg (2lb 4oz) white potatoes, such as Maris Piper left unpeeled and chopped into large bite-sized pieces

120ml (½ cup) good olive oil

3 tbsp (⅓ cup) fine semolina

2 tsp dried oregano, plus extra to serve

200g (7oz) feta, crumbled

50g (½ cup) green olives, pitted and roughly chopped

sea salt

Par-boil the potatoes in a large pot of boiling salted water for 10–15 minutes, until the outside is tender but they're still slightly firm in the middle. Drain the potatoes, then tip them into a large roasting tin and leave to cool slightly for about 20 minutes. Drizzle the still-warm potatoes with about two-thirds of the olive oil, making sure they are evenly coated, before leaving them to cool completely.

Heat the oven to 180°C fan (400°F/Gas 6).

Mix the semolina and oregano in a bowl and season with salt. Tip the mixture over the potatoes and give them a shake in the tin to roughen up the edges and to help a crust form on the outside as they roast.

Pour the rest of the olive oil over the potatoes and roast for 45 minutes. Halfway through give the tin a shake so the potatoes become evenly crisp and golden. Pile the potatoes into a serving bowl, then scatter over the feta and olives. Season with salt and a little oregano. Serve with the fish at the table.

Cherry and Apricot Tart

Apricots develop an intensely aromatic, almost floral flavour, when they're roasted, and pair so well with tart cherries and almonds in this soured-cream custard tart. This is truly one of the easiest desserts to make and you can prepare it well in advance of the rest of the menu. I'm very lazy when it comes to pastry and tend to use ready-made, which is a good alternative, especially the all-butter ones.

375g (13oz) ready-rolled all-butter shortcrust (pie crust) pastry

200ml (scant 1 cup) full-fat crème fraîche

1 whole egg

1 egg yolk

80g (½ cup minus 2 tsp) caster (superfine) sugar

100g (1 cup) ground almonds

1 tsp cornflour (cornstarch)

¼ tsp finely grated unwaxed lemon zest

a pinch of sea salt

1 tsp vanilla paste or extract

2–3 small ripe apricots, stoned and quartered

150g (1 cup) red cherries, halved and pitted

icing (confectioners') sugar, to dust

double (heavy) cream, to serve

Heat the oven to 180°C fan (400°F/Gas 6).

Place the pastry in a 23cm (9in) fluted tart tin, then press it into the base and up the sides so that it fills all the grooves. Trim the excess pastry from the top with a sharp knife. Line the pastry with a piece of baking (parchment) paper and fill with baking beans or rice to weigh it down as it cooks. Bake for 20 minutes, until light golden around the edges.

Carefully take the tart out of the oven, remove the baking beans and paper, and return the pastry case to the oven to cook the base for 5 minutes.

While the pastry case is baking, whisk the crème fraîche, whole egg and egg yolk with the sugar, ground almonds, cornflour, lemon zest, salt and vanilla in a jug or bowl.

Carefully pour the custard mix into the pastry case. Arrange the apricots and cherries on top and bake for 35 minutes, until the custard is set and the fruit peeking through is lightly golden.

Leave the tart to cool and dust generously with icing sugar before serving with cream.

Gnudi in Toasted Lemon-Thyme Butter

Gnudi means "naked" in Italian and partly for that reason these traditional Tuscan ricotta dumplings always feel like a sexy and special thing to make. As soft and delicate as anything can be, these pillowy dumplings are worth the time they take. As the gnudi chill out in a container of fine semolina it creates a protective shell that prevents the fragile filling from falling apart during cooking. It doesn't matter if the gnudi aren't uniform in shape; the magic of dusting off the semolina and seeing them transformed makes this dish so much fun. I like to serve them in a simple sauce, and this toasted lemon and thyme butter is perfect, especially with a cloud of Parmesan on top.

250g (1 cup minus 1 tbsp) ricotta

1 egg, lightly beaten

a pinch of freshly grated nutmeg

½ tsp sea salt

2 tbsp finely grated Parmesan cheese, plus extra to serve

1 tsp finely grated unwaxed lemon zest

1 tbsp plain (all-purpose) flour

600g (4 cups) fine semolina

70g (4½ tbsp) salted butter

½ tsp thyme leaves

freshly ground black pepper

LEFTOVER SEMOLINA

Save the leftover semolina that the gnudi were chilling in for dusting potatoes before you roast them, in the same way as the Crispy Potatoes With Oregano, Olives and Feta (see p.127).

Line a sieve with muslin (cheesecloth) or a clean tea towel and spoon in the ricotta. Gather the cloth around the ricotta and squeeze out as much liquid as you can (it needs to have little to no liquid in it so take your time with this). Tip the ricotta into a large mixing bowl and add the egg, nutmeg, salt, Parmesan, half the lemon zest and the flour and mix together until smooth.

Pour 200g (1⅓ cups) of the semolina onto a large plate. Scoop out a heaped tablespoon of the ricotta mix, drop it into the semolina to roughly coat, then gently roll it between the palms of your hands into a round dumpling. Don't worry if the gnudi is a bit uneven, cracked, or misshaped at this point – you'll get to roll it again before cooking. Repeat this process until the ricotta mix is used and you've got 12 little gnudi.

Fill a large lidded container with another 200g (1⅓ cups) of the semolina and the leftovers from the rolling plate. Nestle each gnudi into the semolina, spaced apart so they're not touching. Pour the remaining semolina over the top until they are almost submerged. Cover with the lid and chill for at least 5 hours, turning the gnudi halfway through.

When you're ready to cook the gnudi, put a large pot of salted water on to boil.

Meanwhile, make the sauce. Add the butter, the remaining lemon zest and the thyme to a small pan and turn the heat to medium-high. Cook for about 5 minutes, until the butter starts to foam and becomes deep golden, then turn the heat off.

Once the water comes to the boil, turn the heat down to a gentle simmer. Lift 6 gnudi out of the semolina, roll them a little in your hands to shape into perfect spheres, and very carefully lower them into the simmering water. Cook for about 4 minutes, until the gnudi float to the surface. Gently nudge the gnudi with the edge of a wooden spoon as they cook to make sure they don't stick to the bottom of the pot. Scoop them out of the water with a slotted spoon and keep warm while you cook the remaining gnudi.

Place 6 gnudi in each serving bowl. Spoon over the lemon-thyme butter, season with pepper and top with extra Parmesan.

Just to Delight

Braised Beans With Roasted Pumpkin and Sage

This is the sort of dish you want to eat when the first hint of autumn is in the air, the sun starts to set early and all you want to wear is something warm. Pumpkin and sage are a perfect pairing, and when combined with comforting white beans they really shine. White wine and stock are at the base of the sauce, but if you want to turn this dish into something closer to a soup, simply double the amount of stock or water. Watching the sage leaves curl as they fry in the butter is so satisfying, and looking at many of the recipes in this book is something that I like to do quite often. When you drizzle the sage butter over the beans at the end, you'll want to eat them with a spoon straightaway. If you can wait though, cover them with grated Parmesan and you'll be even happier. I like to serve the beans alongside Italian fennel sausages, roast chicken, or with more stock as a soup with some leafy greens added at the end, but I think they'd be good with almost anything.

300g (10½oz) pumpkin or squash of choice, deseeded and sliced

a few good glugs of olive oil

a drizzle of runny honey

1 garlic clove, minced

1 rosemary sprig, finely chopped, stalk removed

450g (1lb) (drained weight) jarred/canned white beans or butterbeans (lima), rinsed

200ml (scant 1 cup) white wine

200ml (scant 1 cup) vegetable/chicken stock or water

2 tbsp finely chopped parsley leaves

a pinch of freshly grated nutmeg

1 tbsp salted butter

a few sage leaves

sea salt and freshly ground black pepper

plenty of freshly grated Parmesan cheese, to serve

Heat the oven to 180°C fan (400°F/Gas 6) and line a baking tray with baking (parchment) paper. Toss the pumpkin or squash in a glug of olive oil, place on the lined tray and roast for 35 minutes, until tender. In the last 5 minutes of roasting, cover the pumpkin with a good drizzle of honey and season with salt and pepper. Put the pumpkin back in the oven to caramelize a little, then leave to cool.

Five minutes before the pumpkin is ready, pour a good glug of olive oil into a large pan and add the garlic and rosemary. Place on a medium-high heat and let the garlic and rosemary sizzle in the oil until fragrant. Add the beans and stir to coat them in the flavoured oil. Pour in the wine and let it sizzle for a couple of minutes to burn off some of the booze, then add the stock or water.

Turn the heat down a little and stir in the roasted pumpkin, put the lid on and simmer for 15 minutes, until the liquid has reduced a little. You can use a wooden spoon to crush some of the beans and pumpkin to help thicken the sauce. Add the parsley and nutmeg, then season with salt and pepper to taste.

In a small frying pan, melt the butter. Add the sage and cook until the leaves crisp in the browning butter. When you're ready to eat, pour the butter and crispy sage leaves over the beans, then spoon into 2 bowls (or serve as a side dish) and cover with lots of freshly grated Parmesan.

The Importance of Oysters

Oysters are an omen of all good things where I come from. In the rock pools beneath my parents' house in Sydney, oysters cling to everything. Their taste encapsulates the ocean: like the moment a wave crashes against your ankles at the beach and mists you in salty air; or the feeling of floating in a sea pool, tasting the saltwater on your tongue as you lick your lips. For most of my life, I've lived away from Australia and the house that I call home, but when eating an oyster, I feel like I'm back there in an instant.

What were once seen as a cheap snack given out for free in London pubs to lure in customers, oysters are now considered the epitome of luxury. In my eyes, oysters are saved to mark a special occasion, they're a celebration in a shell, and the start of so many meals that have mattered most to me throughout my life. I wouldn't want to eat them on a mundane Monday no matter how much I love them, it's because I only eat them a few times a year that they remain singular in their meaning to me.

A few years ago, I spent my first Christmas away from my parents. I was 24, my grandfather had passed away a few weeks before, leaving my family heartbroken, and I was dating a string of some of London's most terrible men. I couldn't have been less looking forward to spending Christmas in the city on my own, and so my best friend, Maddi, came over from New York and we vowed to make it one to remember forever. Before her flight had even left JFK, I had written the menus for everything we were going to cook and eat together on her visit.

I had decided early on that the only way to keep the weight of horrible homesickness at bay that Christmas was to eat oysters. Neither of us had the budget to go out somewhere fancy for dinner and order them, so having them at home was the only option. On Christmas Eve, we queued at the fishmongers, Steve Hatt in Islington, with what felt like hundreds of others, and I bought a dozen oysters with the determination that I'd be able to shuck them myself.

Shucking oysters should come with a safety warning; it's one of those fabled kitchen tasks that cooks speak about in hushed tones as they retell stories of when it has gone wrong and swap scars. With this in mind, I was terrified as I stared at the dozen slate-grey shells in front of me and the old Ikea paring knife I thought would do the trick. A chef I was dating at the time doubted me: did I have an oyster knife he asked. A metal glove? I had neither, but by the time I was two glasses of fizz down, trying not to cry listening to Crowded House, as Maddi used a rolling pin to crush ice on the balcony outside, I was ready. Twenty minutes later, we were looking at a platter of oysters balanced on ice that looked like it could have come out of a posh restaurant kitchen. It's the proudest I've ever been of anything I've ever served, and nothing even needed cooking. I promise that the satisfaction of shucking your own oysters is more than making any dish in this book ten times over.

So much has been written about the romance of oysters, and Maddi and I felt it that night as we shared the platter of them before eating prawns and finally pavlova - it's still a dinner we talk about today. Always risk the fear of failure when the result could be delight.

How to Shuck an Oyster

1. Fold a clean tea towel in half, then in half again lengthways and wrap half of it around your less dominant hand.

2. Hold and tightly grip the oyster flat in the towel making sure that it remains level the whole time with the hinge of the oyster facing away from you.

3. Nudge the tip of the knife into the hinge that joins both sides of the shell and wiggle and twist the knife in to prise the shell open.

4. Clean the knife, then use it to disconnect the oyster from its shell; try to keep the shell upright so you don't lose any of the lovely seawater inside.

5. Arrange the oysters on a platter of crushed ice, so they're nice and cold.

6. Bring lots of black pepper, your champagne mignonette (*see p.136*) and plenty of lemon wedges to the table, ready to serve.

Oysters and Champagne Mignonette

Preparing oysters is an occasion in itself; you can find oyster knives pretty cheaply, but a small, sturdy paring knife does the trick too. Throw your own oyster happy hour at home complete with a champagne mignonette – just don't drink too much champagne before you start shucking.

12 oysters

plenty of crushed ice, to serve

CHAMPAGNE MIGNONETTE

2 tbsp very finely chopped shallot

125ml (½ cup) red wine vinegar

a splash of champagne or sparkling wine

A few hours before you want to serve the oysters, make the champagne mignonette. Mix the shallot and vinegar and leave to infuse until ready to serve.

Shuck the oysters (*see p.133*) and place on a serving platter covered with crushed ice.

Right before you serve, add a splash of fizz to the mignonette and spoon a little over each oyster before eating.

A Soothing Sunday Lunch

Relax on the sofa as your chicken roasts, and potatoes bubble away in cream. This is a meal that largely takes care of itself, leaving you free to do whatever you fancy.

A Tiny Cheeseboard • A Proper Roast Chicken • Potato and Fennel Gratin • Green Leaves and Lemon-Jam Dressing • Chocolate Profiteroles

---

Comfort and romance are sometimes one and the same and, for me, true romance is sharing a roast chicken. It's the dish I serve to woo someone that I know I'll love; it's the first thing I cooked for my best friend, Maddi. Falling in love with a friend is a special sort of love. At the time she was a broke actress living above a pub in Hampstead, London, surviving on bread rolls from the back of the kitchen, and I was living alone wishing I had someone to cook for. She says that she knew I'd be in her life forever when she hugged me as I was cooking, and I smelt like chicken fat. I say I knew when I watched her reach for the crispiest bit of chicken skin at the end of the meal, making sure that not one bit was left to go to waste. It's that element of sharing a roast chicken with someone that I love the most.

I roast a chicken every Sunday without fail. The routine is often a way to remedy the anxieties that sometimes come with the start of a new week, and to find a bit of comfort in the kitchen. I never tire of its familiarity: the herbs I stir into the softened butter, and the sprinkle of salt to ensure a crisp skin are memorized in my muscles. Joe and I share it for lunch with some sort of potatoes - home-made chips or roast potatoes, if he's choosing, or something with lots of cream if I am - and we linger at the table until the bottle of wine is empty and there's nothing left but bones. Joe does the dishes, I start the stock, and we take turns checking on it as it simmers while we go about the rest of our afternoon.

I have made roast chicken a thousand different ways, but this one is inspired by the world's most perfect roast chicken at restaurant Allard in Paris. It's served for two to share in a pool of hot melted butter and although sides come with it, once you taste the chicken you won't remember what they are; the chicken is the star as it should be. Inspired by both this as well as the rotisserie chicken sold in French markets, where you get to choose the flavour of the herbed butter for basting, I prefer to opt for a single herb to fragrance the butter, which is slipped under the skin of the chicken before roasting.

I like to keep my side dishes simple and tend to go with a gorgeously dressed crisp green salad and something rich like a gratin and, of course, some cheese to snack on while the chicken roasts. This is a menu to make for those times when you're still picking the chicken meat off the carcass over a second bottle of wine in the comfort of your pyjamas in the knowledge that you're with someone you could stay up all night talking to.

A Tiny Cheeseboard

Sometimes all you need is a tiny cheeseboard. It's a sort-of-starter, sort-of-snack that will keep you and your guest occupied as the chicken roasts and the potatoes cook in the oven. Choose your favourite cheese, something sweet, something salty, a little crunch perhaps and, of course, a carb. Select one from each of the columns (right), or stay simple, because there are no rules to say that a wheel of ripe Camembert and a jar of runny honey with a warm baguette aren't enough to be a cheeseboard. Be intentional with your choices as long you've got all the key elements.

Cheese	Fruit	Carb	Something Salty	Finishing Touch
Super-soft cheese (goat's cheese or marinated feta)	Grapes	Crackers	Caper berries	Chutney
Hard cheese (Parmesan or Manchego)	Pear	Torn up focaccia	Cornichons	Quince paste
Blue cheese (Gorgonzola or Stilton)	Figs	Toasted crostini	Parma ham	Honey
Soft cheese (Brie or Camembert)	Apricots	Warm baguette	Olives	Jam

A Proper Roast Chicken

A good free-range chicken, fancy salted butter and a big bunch of aromatic herbs make this a dish that you won't forget. I like to stick to a single type of herb because I love to focus on the simplicity of flavour when combined with the butter and chicken fat, although you can use a mix if you fancy.

1.5kg (3lb 3oz) free-range chicken

a small bunch of your choice of herb (I like thyme, tarragon, chervil or parsley)

45g (3 tbsp) salted butter, softened

1 unwaxed lemon

1 tbsp Dijon mustard

a drizzle of olive oil

1 large onion, cut in half

sea salt and freshly ground black pepper

An hour or so before you want to roast your chicken, take it out of the packaging, pat the skin dry with kitchen paper (paper towels), and place it in a large roasting tin. Let the chicken come to room temperature.

Chop about 1 tablespoon of your herb of choice (leaving the rest whole) into the soft butter. Finely grate the zest of the lemon and add half to the herb butter, then season with plenty of salt and pepper, and mix in the Dijon mustard. Using your fingers, separate the chicken skin from the breast. Push the lemon and herb butter under the skin, being careful not to tear it. You can add a few whole sprigs of the herb, too, if you fancy. As the chicken cooks and the skin crisps, it will become glass-like and the herbs will show through.

Heat the oven to 200°C fan (425°F/Gas 7). Chop the lemon in half, put it inside the chicken cavity and season generously with salt and pepper. Drizzle a little olive oil over the chicken, making sure it is covered, then season all over with salt and pepper. Place the onion halves, cut-side down, in the tin and put the chicken on top. Pour 150ml (2/3 cup) water into the bottom of the tin, add the rest of the lemon zest and any remaining herbs.

Roast the chicken for 20 minutes. Turn the oven down to 180°C fan (400°F/Gas 6) and roast for another hour, basting the chicken with the herb butter in the bottom of the tin every 10 minutes or so. Check the chicken is cooked by making sure the juices run clear when you pull the legs away from the breast. Cover the chicken with foil and let it rest on a warm plate for at least 20 minutes.

Pour the buttery pan juices out of the roasting tin into a pan, skim some of the fat off the top, and cook over a medium-high heat for 10 minutes, until reduced.

Carve the chicken and spoon over the reduced pan juices to serve alongside the gratin and green salad.

Potato and Fennel Gratin

On nights when I'm home alone, I've been known to make this potato and fennel gratin just for me for dinner – that's how much I love this dish. It might seem like a lot of effort, but really once you've peeled and thinly sliced the potatoes, you're pretty much done.

1 tbsp salted butter

1 fennel bulb, cut in half, tough outer layer removed, thinly sliced

200ml (scant 1 cup) single (light) cream

a pinch of freshly grated nutmeg

1 tsp sea salt

¼ tsp freshly ground black pepper

2 garlic cloves, finely grated

2 tbsp finely grated Parmesan cheese

2 large floury potatoes, about 500g in total, peeled and thinly sliced using a mandoline or small sharp knife

1 bay leaf

Heat the oven to 180°C fan (400°F/Gas 6).

Melt the butter in a frying pan over a medium heat, add the fennel and sauté for 6–8 minutes, until softened and it starts to colour.

In a bowl, mix the cream, nutmeg, salt, pepper, garlic and 1 tablespoon of the Parmesan. Pour a little of the cream mix into the bottom of a gratin dish, about 20cm (8in) in diameter, then top with a layer of potato slices – they can slightly overlap at the edges – a layer of fennel, another layer of potatoes and pour over some of the cream mix until the dish is filled halfway. Pop the bay leaf in the middle of the dish. Keep layering the fennel, potato and cream mix until you've used up all the ingredients – there should be 5 layers in total, ending with a layer of potato. Sprinkle the rest of the Parmesan over the top.

Bake for 1 hour (put the gratin in the oven 20 minutes after you reduce the temperature roasting the chicken), until the potatoes are tender and the top of the gratin is golden and bubbling.

Green Leaves and Lemon-Jam Dressing

It may be a side salad, but it should still feel special, and this one certainly does. There are two key factors to a truly sublime green salad and that's super crisp leaves and a dressing that is so good you want to eat it with a spoon. I've been making this dressing for years and always have a jar of it at home because it's so versatile. It's the best because it's also amazing on roasted vegetables, particularly tomatoes or fennel; drizzled over a slab of baked feta; or spooned over sliced avocado.

an assortment of green salad leaves, such as romaine, butterhead and frisee, washed, left in iced water for 5 minutes to crisp up, then drained well

1 lemon, cut in half

½ garlic clove, finely grated

½ tsp Dijon mustard

75ml (5 tbsp) extra-virgin olive oil

½ tsp sea salt

a tiny pinch of sugar

To make the dressing, heat a dry, heavy-based pan or cast-iron skillet over a medium-high heat. Place the lemon, cut-side down, in the pan and let it char and caramelize for around 5 minutes, until deep brown and almost black in places. Turn the heat down to low and cook the lemon, still cut-side down, for another 15 minutes, until the outside of the flesh is burnished and the inside is soft and jammy. Remove the pan from the heat and let the lemon cool in the pan. Once cool enough to handle, squeeze the juice and jammy pulp into a bowl.

Pick out any lemon seeds before adding the garlic (the lemon should still be a little warm, which will take the edge off the raw garlic), mustard, olive oil and salt and whisk till combined. Taste and add the smallest pinch of sugar to round off the flavour; this all depends on your lemon and may not be needed.

Roughly tear the salad leaves in a serving bowl, add a few spoonfuls of the dressing and toss gently before serving alongside your roast chicken and pototo and fennel gratin.

Chocolate Profiteroles

In the list of my top five desserts (something that is a work in progress), profiteroles are always in the top three. If they're on a dessert menu, everything else becomes irrelevant to me. I don't really discriminate and love all profiteroles in different ways, but the chef Jeremy Lee's at Quo Vardis in London, which come filled with scoops of vanilla ice-cream and topped with hot chocolate sauce, are the epitome of excellence. Here is my version, inspired by Jeremy, and filled with ice cream. To help the choux pastry be as light as air, run your hands under cold water before quickly rolling each bun between your palms; the water creates steam and helps them to rise, ensuring they remain perfectly round. Make the profiteroles the morning of your lunch and leave them covered with a clean tea towel on a baking tray until you've eaten the chicken, then whip up the hot chocolate sauce to serve with them. I like to serve three per person; the recipe makes eight so the other two are importantly the cook's bonus.

PROFITEROLES

70g (½ cup) plain (all-purpose) flour

2 tsp icing (confectioners') sugar

a generous pinch of fine sea salt

60g (4 tbsp) cold salted butter

120ml (½ cup) whole milk

2 eggs

1 tsp vanilla extract

a tub of vanilla ice cream, to serve

HOT CHOCOLATE SAUCE

100g (3½oz) 70% plain (semisweet) chocolate, broken into pieces

100ml (6½ tbsp) double (heavy) cream

a splash of whole milk

a pinch of sea salt, plus extra to finish

To make the choux pastry, sift the flour, icing sugar and salt together in a bowl and stir until combined.

In a medium pot, melt the butter in the milk on a medium heat and whisk to combine. Turn the heat up and just as the milk starts to boil, pour in the flour mix. Using a wooden spoon, vigorously beat for 1–2 minutes, until the mixture forms a shiny ball of dough that comes away from the sides of the pot. Take the pot off the heat and tip the dough into a mixing bowl.

Spread the dough up the sides of the bowl to help it cool. Let the dough sit for 5 minutes and as it cools slightly, beat the eggs with the vanilla in a separate bowl. Using an electric whisk, a spatula or wooden spoon, mix the eggs and vanilla mixture into the dough, a third at a time. Be quick: once you've added the first third, stir the dough like mad. Every time you add the eggs, you'll feel like you've ruined it – fear not, keep stirring – until it forms a glossy dough. Chill for 30 minutes or up to 1 hour.

Heat the oven to 200°C fan (425°F/Gas 7) and line a baking tray with baking (parchment) paper.

Scoop out 2 tablespoons of the dough, about 40g (1½oz) per bun, and with wet hands, roll the dough into a small, round ball. Repeat to make 8 balls in total and place them on the lined tray, equally spaced apart to allow the buns room to double in size. Bake for 20–25 minutes, until the buns have ballooned in size and are hollow sounding when tapped underneath. Place the buns on a cooling rack to cool completely.

To make the hot chocolate sauce, in a double boiler or heatproof bowl set over a pan of gently simmering water, melt the chocolate with the double cream. Stir in a splash of milk to give an easy pouring consistency and the salt to increase the intensity of the chocolate flavour. (You can make the sauce in advance, then carefully melt it again over a double boiler when ready to serve.) Pour the hot sauce into a jug and serve at the table.

Slice the profiteroles in half and fill each one with a small tablespoon-sized scoop of vanilla ice cream. Arrange on a platter and pour over the hot chocolate sauce at the table, sprinkling the profiteroles with a little extra sea salt, if you like.

Sunday Night Soup

I like to stay home on a Sunday. Saturday is the day for shopping, pottering and exploring London, but on Sunday things slow down and we stay in. A long, lingering breakfast leads to taking it in turns to chop onions and peel potatoes to start our regular A Proper Roast Chicken lunch (*see p.140*). By the time the sun starts to set, the stock for this soup, made from the leftover chicken carcass, has already been simmering for a few hours and has usually steamed up the windows in the flat. It's during those hours on a late Sunday afternoon that I really switch off. Knowing that dinner is sorting itself, we get on with other things as the gentle hum of the stove soundtracks everything.

You can make a version of this soup with pre-made stock and poached chicken, but it's really good made with the carcass of my roast chicken, as it takes on all the lovely flavour of the bones, butter, lemon and herbs, which impart the best of everything into your stock. Plus, I hate seeing anything go to waste, so for that reason alone I pair the two recipes together. I use variations of tiny pasta shapes, like orzo or ditalini, but I adore watching the star-shaped stelline shimmer in the hot broth.

STOCK

1 roast chicken carcass and any leftover meat

1 bay leaf

½ tsp black peppercorns

½ tsp fennel seeds

½ brown onion

1 carrot, cut into 3 pieces

2 celery stalks, snapped in half

½ fennel bulb, sliced

SOUP

1 tbsp olive oil

200g (7oz) dried stelline

a pinch of sea salt

finely grated zest of ½ unwaxed lemon

juice of 1 lemon

a pinch of ground cinnamon

1 garlic clove, finely grated

1 small bunch of dill, roughly chopped

dried chilli flakes (crushed red pepper flakes), for sprinkling

Remove the meat from the leftover chicken carcass and place in a bowl to use later in the soup. Put the carcass in the largest pot you've got and pour over 3 litres (12²/₃ cups) cold water. Add the bay leaf, peppercorns, fennel seeds, onion, carrot, celery and fennel.

Place the pot on the stove and turn the heat to high. Once boiling, turn the heat to low so the stock gently simmers. Let it simmer for 3–4 hours with the lid off, then take it off the heat to cool a little. Place a large fine colander or sieve over another large pot and strain the stock – you should have about 1.5 litres (6¼ cups) – and discard the carcass and other solids. Leave the stock to cool if not using straightaway; you can also make it ahead and freeze, or pop it in the fridge for a day or two.

When you're ready to make the soup, heat the olive oil in a heavy-bottomed pot on a medium heat. Pour in the stelline and fry until lightly golden, stirring so each star catches a little colour. Just as you start to smell the pasta toasting, ladle in about 1 litre (4¹/₃ cups) of the stock until the pasta is covered and starts to simmer. Stir in the leftover chicken meat and salt and simmer for 6–7 minutes, until the pasta is cooked.

Take the soup off the heat and add the lemon zest and juice. Stir in the cinnamon, garlic and half the dill. Spoon the soup into 2 bowls and top with the rest of the dill and a sprinkle of chilli flakes.

Just to Delight

Attilio's Schnitzel and Spaghetti

The longer you live in one place, the more certain streets and shop fronts haunt you. Every time I walk down Cowcross Street in Clerkenwell, I stop and stand outside what used to be Attilio's restaurant. When I first moved to London, my best friend, Maddi, and I were tempted by its sandwich-board sign advertising three courses for £9.99, which importantly included a glass of prosecco. Each table was covered in a wipe-clean, red-and-white gingham tablecloth. Breadsticks and salty olives were set in front of you the second you sat down, and the waiters would top up your glass of free fizz all night. The walls of the tiny restaurant were painted with the owner's face across a myriad of murals; in one, he was a fisherman, in another he was a king, and so on.

As years went by, it became somewhere I always went to for comfort, a familiar face, and to order the same meal – schnitzel and spaghetti, finished with curly parsley and plenty of Parmesan. It was perfect. Now, don't get me wrong, I know that it wasn't the best version of this dish, but it was something about the setting. On my third date with Joe, we went and ordered the schnitzel and spaghetti, but 2 weeks later Attilio's closed forever. This is my version of the beloved combination that will always make me miss those murals.

SPAGHETTI AND TOMATO SAUCE

½ white onion, finely chopped

1 tsp salted butter

1 tsp tomato purée (tomato paste)

2 garlic cloves, finely chopped

400ml (1¾ cups) passata

a pinch of dried chilli flakes (crushed red pepper flakes)

a pinch of sugar (optional)

¼ tsp sea salt, plus extra to cook the pasta

Parmesan cheese rind if, you have one

200g (7oz) dried spaghetti

2 tbsp chopped basil, plus extra leaves to serve

CHICKEN SCHNITZEL

1 egg, lightly beaten

40g (⅓ cup) plain (all-purpose) flour

45g (1 cup) panko breadcrumbs

finely grated zest of ½ unwaxed lemon

4 tbsp finely grated Parmesan cheese, plus extra to serve

2 skinless, boneless chicken breasts, each halved lengthways to make 4 pieces in total

90ml (6 tbsp) olive oil

1 tbsp butter

sea salt and freshly ground black pepper

1 lemon, cut into wedges, to serve

First make the tomato sauce. Add the onion to a large, heavy-bottomed pot with the butter. Cook on a medium heat for 5 minutes, until the onion is soft and translucent.

Add the tomato purée and cook for 1 minute before stirring in the garlic. When the garlic is fragrant, pour in the passata and 200ml (scant 1 cup) water. Gives everything a stir and add the chilli, sugar, salt and the Parmesan rind, if using.

When the sauce starts to bubble, turn the heat down to low and simmer, uncovered, for 30 minutes, stirring every so often so the sauce doesn't stick.

While the sauce is simmering, make the schnitzel. Heat the oven to 160°C fan (350°F/Gas 4).

Beat the egg in a shallow bowl and season with salt and pepper. Tip the flour onto a plate and season with salt and pepper. Place the panko breadcrumbs on a second plate, stir in the lemon zest and Parmesan, then season with salt and pepper.

Lay the chicken pieces on top of a chopping board and season with salt and pepper. Place a sheet of baking (parchment) paper on top, then using the end of a rolling pin, flatten each one until about 5mm (¼in) thick.

Take out one piece of the chicken and place in the seasoned flour, then turn to lightly coat both sides. Next, dip the chicken in the egg, making sure every bit is covered before transferring it to the breadcrumb mixture. Use your fingers to press the crumbs into the chicken to form a thick crust, then place the crumbed chicken breast on a plate as you repeat the process to coat all 4 pieces.

Meanwhile, put a large pot of salted water on to cook the pasta.

To cook the chicken schnitzels, heat the oil and butter in a large frying pan on a medium-high heat. To check it's hot enough, drop a single breadcrumb into the pan and if it sizzles and turns light golden, then you're ready to fry. Cook 2 chicken breast pieces at a time for 2 minutes on each side, until golden. When all 4 pieces have been fried, place them on a baking (parchment) paper-lined baking tray, sprinkle with salt and place in the oven for 10 minutes to keep hot and crisp.

When the pasta water comes to the boil, add the spaghetti and cook following the instructions on the packet. Drain, reserving a ladleful of the cooking water.

Add the spaghetti and cooking water to the tomato sauce (first removing the Parmesan rind, if using). Add the basil and toss until combined.

Serve the chicken schnitzel with a side of tomato spaghetti, topped with plenty of extra Parmesan and basil leaves, and lemon wedges on the side for squeezing over the chicken.

Truffle Tagliatelle

I couldn't tell you when it was, or the reason we went there that night but, of course, I can remember everything about the plate of pasta I ate. There's a restaurant in Sydney called Buon Riccordo, an Italian institution famous for one special dish: fresh truffle pasta tossed at the table with a barely cooked fried egg and a large amount of Parmesan. It's obscenely rich and just a few forkfuls may be enough for some, but I could probably devour two servings, it's that good. It's a dish that I've thought about for years and something I've never seen on a menu in London, so for a special occasion when restaurants were closed a few years ago, I had a go at recreating a version at home.

The romance of the dish lies in its decadence – a fresh black truffle is not an everyday ingredient, but there is nothing quite like it. I occasionally now make this dish for special occasions; instead of going out for dinner I head to Borough Market in London to buy a black truffle. You can get a tiny one that's more than enough to make this dish (and truffle scrambled eggs for breakfast the next morning). The sauce is an amalgamation of egg yolks, cheese, butter, black truffle and pasta cooking water, which helps to emulsify the sauce. A lightly dressed green salad and a glass of something special are the only extras you need.

45g (1½oz) Parmesan cheese, finely grated, plus extra to serve

3 egg yolks

1 whole egg

a pinch of freshly grated nutmeg

a generous pinch of sea salt

a tiny pinch of ground white pepper

1 whole black truffle, about 15g (½oz) in total

200g (7oz) fresh tagliatelle

15g (1 tbsp) salted butter

freshly ground black pepper

Mix the Parmesan with the egg yolks, whole egg, nutmeg, salt and white pepper. Using a fine grater, grate half of the truffle and stir it into the egg mix.

Cook the tagliatelle in a big pot of boiling salted water following the packet instructions. Just before the tagliatelle is ready, scoop out a small ladleful of the pasta cooking water and quickly stir it into the egg and truffle mix.

Drain the pasta, keeping a mugful of pasta water to one side.

Return the pasta to the pot, pour over the egg mix and add the butter. Quickly toss to combine until the egg mix has emulsified into the most divine sauce, clinging to the tagliatelle. Keep stirring everything together and, if you think it needs it, add more pasta water to the sauce until it has a gorgeous, velvety consistency.

Pile the pasta onto 2 plates and cover with more finely grated Parmesan and wafer-thin slices of truffle. Season with freshly ground black pepper.

Slow-Cooked Lamb and Cinnamon Stew

This is the sort of dish you cook when you feel weighed down by the world and you want to retreat from it all with a bowl of something soothing. It's the type of dish Mum would make on a weeknight during winter – just one spoonful would make me feel that no matter what had happened during the day, everything would be alright. Inspired by one of my all-time favourite things to eat, Greek stifado with cinnamon, red wine and oregano, it fills the kitchen with an aroma better than any scented candle. With a handful of salty olives and creamy white beans added at the end, it brings everything together to make this stew the main event of any evening. As the stew slowly simmers over 3½ hours, the sauce reduces and the lamb becomes meltingly tender. It also freezes like a dream: simply double the recipe to have a stew waiting for you on a rainy day when you need it most.

500g (1lb 2oz) diced lamb (I like to use leg or shoulder)

4 tbsp olive oil

½ large white onion, finely chopped

2 garlic cloves, finely chopped

½ tsp dried oregano

1 tbsp tomato purée (tomato paste)

200ml (scant 1 cup) red wine

1 small cinnamon stick

½ tsp dried chilli flakes (crushed red pepper flakes)

1 bay leaf

a small strip of unwaxed lemon peel

400ml (1¾ cups) passata .

1 handful of black olives, about 15, pitted

300g white beans from a jar, drained

100g (3½oz) feta, crumbled

1 handful of roughly chopped parsley, or leaves left whole

sea salt and freshly ground black pepper

Start by generously seasoning the lamb with salt and pepper. In a large, heavy-bottomed pot, heat the olive oil on a medium-high heat and fry the lamb in batches, a third at a time, until golden brown all over. Remove the lamb from the pot with a slotted spoon and put on a plate to one side.

Add the onion to the pot and fry in the olive oil and lamb fat for a few minutes or until it starts to colour, then add the garlic. When the onion and garlic have softened, add the oregano and tomato purée and cook for 2–3 minutes, until everything starts to caramelize and catch on the bottom of the pot.

Pour in the red wine to deglaze the pot, making sure you scrape all the good bits from the bottom. Add the cinnamon, chilli, bay leaf and lemon peel, then return the lamb to the pot. Pour in the passata and 400ml (1¾ cups) water and stir until combined. Pop on the lid and simmer for 3 hours on a low heat, stirring every now and then to make sure it's not sticking on the bottom.

Take the lid off for the last 30 minutes of cooking and add the olives and white beans. Stir everything together and continue to cook until heated through.

Spoon the stew into 2 bowls and scatter over the crumbled feta and parsley before serving.

Stuffed Cabbage Leaves

This dish is just as calming to cook as it is to eat; I love the ritual of making it together before you put it in the oven to bake. Filling and folding the leaves inside a ladle is a technique taught to me by the gorgeous Bulgarian chef, Aleksandar Taralezhkov, when I interviewed him for the opening of his restaurant in London. The dish of stuffed cabbage rolls can historically be traced back thousands of years, and is found in cuisines across the globe. This version has a filling of crispy lamb with toasted pine nuts and plenty of herbs.

6 large Savoy cabbage leaves

4 bay leaves

LAMB AND HERB FILLING

400g (1lb) minced (ground) lamb

1 tsp sea salt, plus extra to season sauce

½ tsp freshly ground black pepper

1 white onion, finely chopped

3 garlic cloves, finely chopped

1 tbsp tomato purée (tomato paste)

½ tsp ground allspice

60g (scant ½ cup) pine nuts

180g (1 cup) short-grain rice, rinsed

½ tsp finely grated unwaxed lemon zest

juice of 1 lemon

4 tbsp finely chopped dill, plus extra to serve

2 tbsp finely chopped parsley

SPICED TOMATO SAUCE

400ml (1¾ cups) passata

1 bay leaf

1 cinnamon stick

¼ tsp dried chilli (crushed red pepper) flakes

1 tbsp salted butter

YOGURT SAUCE

125ml (½ cup) plain yogurt

1 garlic clove, finely grated

juice of 1 lemon

Place the cabbage leaves in a pot of boiling water, then turn the heat down and simmer, covered, for 2 minutes, until just tender. Remove the leaves from the water with a pair of tongs and set them aside to cool.

To make the lamb filling, season the lamb with the salt and the pepper, then add it to a cold sauté pan and turn the heat to high. You want to get the lamb super crispy so don't stir it for a few minutes to allow it to caramelize and the fat to render. When the lamb starts to turn golden after about 10 minutes, stir, then cook for another 10 minutes, until crisp. Spoon the lamb into a bowl and pour off some of the fat in the pan.

Add the onion to the pan and sauté for 5 minutes in the lamb fat, until translucent. Stir in the garlic, tomato purée, ground allspice and pine nuts and cook for another 2 minutes, until fragrant. Tip in the rice and stir to coat the grains in the onion mix before adding 150ml (⅔ cup) water. Stir everything and simmer for 4 minutes before turning the heat off – the rice will only be part-cooked at this stage. Stir in the lemon zest and juice, dill, parsley and lamb. Let the filling cool for 10 minutes.

Meanwhile, make the sauce. Put all the ingredients in a large, heavy-bottomed pot with 400ml (1¾ cups) water, stir and simmer on a medium-low heat for 30 minutes, stirring every so often, until reduced. Season and let cool.

Heat the oven to 180°C fan (400°F/Gas 6). Spoon a layer of the sauce in the bottom of an ovenproof dish.

Lay the cabbage leaves on a chopping board and cut away the thickest part of the central vein at the base of the leaf. Press a cabbage leaf into the bowl of a ladle and stuff with 3–4 tablespoons of the rice mixture, pressing the filling down. Fold over each side of the cabbage leaf to encase the filling. Place the stuffed leaf, seam-side down, in the dish on top of the layer of tomato sauce. Continue to fill the rest of the cabbage leaves, then place them tightly packed in the dish (you may have some of the filling left over for lunch the next day). Tuck in the bay leaves and pour the rest of the sauce over. Cover with foil and bake for 1 hour, until heated through and bubbling.

Meanwhile, mix all the ingredients for the yogurt sauce and chill. Serve the cabbage with the tomato sauce and the yogurt sauce spooned over the top. Finish with a sprinkling of dill.

Spaghetti and Meatballs

When Lady and the Tramp go to the Italian restaurant, Tony's, in the Disney classic *Lady and the Tramp*, the dingy back alley becomes the setting for one of the most divine dates in cinema history. Between the candle glowing in a wine bottle, breadsticks propped up in a basket, the handwritten menu and the gingham tablecloth blowing in the breeze, it all looks pretty dreamy. There's a good reason why spaghetti and meatballs is a classic in the canon of romantic dishes – it's one that's simply best shared.

Spaghetti with meatballs is all about the balance of the almost-sweet tomato sauce and the intense savouriness of the spicy meatballs. You can pan-fry the meatballs before popping them in the sauce, but the sheer ease and convenience of putting them in the oven to crisp on the outside can't be beaten. Make the meatballs in advance, if you fancy, then just poach them in the sauce before serving.

350g (12oz) lean minced (ground) pork

a splash of olive oil, plus extra for greasing

½ large white onion, finely chopped

½ tsp dried chilli flakes (crushed red pepper flakes)

1 tsp fennel seeds

⅛ tsp freshly ground nutmeg

2 garlic cloves, finely minced

1 slice of white bread, about 50g (1¾oz)

100ml (6½ tbsp) whole milk

1 egg, lightly whisked

2 tbsp finely chopped flat-leaf parsley

1½ tsp sea salt

1 recipe quantity Tomato Sauce *(see p.146)*

250g dried spaghetti

2 tbsp finely grated Parmesan cheese

basil leaves, to serve

Start by making the meatballs. Put the pork in a large mixing bowl and set aside.

Pour a splash of olive oil into a large sauté pan on a medium heat, add the onion, chilli, fennel seeds and nutmeg and cook for a few minutes until the onion is soft and translucent. Stir in the garlic and cook for another minute until fragrant, then take the pan off the heat and let the onion mix cool.

Toast the bread until deep golden, then place in a shallow bowl and pour the milk over. Let the toast soak until softened, then roughly tear into small pieces and add to the bowl containing the pork. Mix in the egg, cooled onion mix, parsley and salt.

Using a tablespoon, scoop out even-sized balls of the pork mix and roll each one in your hands to make 25–30 tiny meatballs, then place on an oiled or lined tray and chill for at least 1 hour.

When you're ready to cook, heat the oven to 180°C fan (400°F/Gas 6). Place the meatballs, spaced out on a lined baking tray, and bake for 25 minutes, until golden brown.

Meanwhile, start the tomato sauce, following the instructions on page 147. Once the meatballs are cooked, transfer them to the sauce and simmer with the lid off for a further 20 minutes, until they take on the flavour of the sauce.

While the sauce is simmering, cook the spaghetti in a big pot of boiling salted water following the packet instructions, then drain and add to the sauce. Toss until combined and serve piled into 2 bowls, topped with the Parmesan and basil leaves.

Beef and Guinness Pie

Growing up, whenever life became a bit overwhelming, I knew I'd find comfort in the kitchen with my Mum. Coming home from school after a bad day, during a rainy winter in Sydney, always meant a pie of some sort for dinner. And if Mum knew that I was feeling gloomy, the pastry on my pie would always be lovingly decorated to make me smile: cut-out hearts, flowers or my name, anything in a bid to make me feel better.

Beef and Guinness is such a classic combination, which I adore. I prefer to use beef cheeks, if I can get them at my butcher's, since they taste good and are always reasonably priced, but they can be tricky to source so braising steak is just as good an option and is perfect for slow cooking. Serve the pie with a big helping of colcannon and a pile of buttery peas and, ideally, more Guinness for the proper pub-lunch feeling. Like Mum, have fun with the pastry shapes – I know it doesn't change the taste of the pie, but, trust me, it really changes how you feel when it arrives at the table.

2 tbsp cornflour (cornstarch)
500g (1lb 2oz) beef cheeks, trimmed and cut into large chunks, or diced braising steak
30g (2 tbsp) salted butter
1 white onion, finely chopped
2 celery stalks, finely diced
2 carrots, cut into large pieces
500ml (generous 2 cups) Guinness
400ml (1¾ cups) beef stock
½ tsp finely chopped thyme leaves
½ tsp finely chopped rosemary
1 bay leaf
1½ tbsp brown sauce
1 egg, beaten
a splash of whole milk
1 ready-rolled sheet of all-butter puff pastry, about 300g (10oz)
sea salt and freshly ground black pepper

Put the cornflour in a shallow bowl and season with lots of salt and pepper. Add the beef and toss until lightly coated all over.

Melt half the butter in a large pot, add about a quarter of the beef and cook until browned all over with a caramelized crust. Remove from the pot with a slotted spoon and set aside on a plate while you brown the rest of the beef, adding more butter when needed. Set aside the beef.

Add the onion and celery to the buttery juices in the pot and sauté for 5 minutes, until softened. Add the carrots and a splash of the Guinness to deglaze, stirring to remove any sticky bits in the bottom, and return the beef to the pot. Pour in the beef stock and the rest of the Guinness and add the herbs. Stir, cover with the lid and simmer on a low heat for 1½ hours. Remove the lid and cook for another 1½ hours, until the meat is very tender, and the sauce has reduced and thickened.

Stir in the brown sauce, add a little more salt, if needed, and season with pepper. Skim off some of the fat on the surface, then pour the stew into a 25 x 20cm (10 x 8in) pie dish and leave to cool.

When ready to bake the pie, heat the oven to 180°C fan (400°F/Gas 6).

Beat the egg with the milk to make an egg wash.

Lay out the pastry sheet on the work top and roll out slightly. Wet the edge of the pie dish with a little water and top with the pastry. Trim the pastry to fit and crimp the edges. Cut out whatever shapes you fancy from any leftover pastry. Brush the pastry with the egg wash and arrange the cut-out shapes on top. Eggwash the shapes and cut a small cross in the middle of the pie to let out steam. Bake the pie for 30–40 minutes, until the pastry is golden and the filling bubbling beneath it.

Best Shared = Steak, Chips and a Bottle of Wine

An old-school steak house dinner that will make you feel that the night is young even when dinner is done.

Crab Cakes • Steak for Two • A Choice of Sauces • Joe's Chips With Tarragon Salt • Creamed Spinach Gratin • Crêpes Suzette

---

When I was a kid, twice a year my Dad and I would make an entire day out of shopping for Mum's birthday and Christmas presents. We'd go to a restaurant with pressed white tablecloths and lots of fancy cutlery and I'd get to order whatever I wanted. Even though we went to different restaurants each year, they always seemed the same: there was always steak on the menu and lots of sides, sauces and desserts with names I couldn't pronounce.

When I first moved to London, we kept the tradition alive at Christmas. By then I was old enough to choose a martini to start and share a bottle of wine with Dad as we ordered and ate matching meals. Those dinners felt so sophisticated, no matter the occasion or the circumstances, there was always something to celebrate.

I don't often cook steak at home, but when I do it's in a bid to recreate moments like those with Dad. I want the tablecloth to be pristine, to wipe away any crumbs on the table between courses and to decant the wine. I know cooking a steak can be daunting, but with a decent hot pan everything is fine.

It's a good idea to make the crab cakes, the creamed spinach, tarragon salt for the chips and the crêpes for the dessert ahead of time, so you can focus on the main event of the night.

Crab Cakes

The first time I ate proper American crab cakes was in an old-school steakhouse in New York, where they arrived as an appetizer the size of a small plate. Mine are inspired by those, but I prefer them a wee bit smaller so they make a light starter to a big meal.

1 egg, lightly beaten

2 tbsp finely chopped parsley, plus extra to serve

1 tbsp finely chopped dill

finely grated zest of ½ unwaxed lemon

½ tsp Old Bay Seasoning spice mix

½ tsp mustard powder

3 tbsp mayonnaise

75g (1 cup) panko breadcrumbs

200g (7oz) white crab meat

120ml (½ cup) oil for frying

sea salt and freshly ground black pepper

lemon wedges, to serve

In a bowl, mix the egg, herbs, lemon zest, spice mix, mustard powder, mayonnaise and 3 heaped tablespoons of the breadcrumbs until combined. Gently fold through the crab meat. Put the remaining breadcrumbs on a plate and season.

Using a tablespoon, scoop out the crab mix and roll into a ball with damp hands. Repeat to make 8 in total. Roll the crab cakes in the breadcrumbs until coated, then place on a plate and chill for 1 hour.

Warm the oil in a large frying pan over a medium heat and shallow fry the crab cakes for 3 minutes on each side until golden. Serve scattered with parsley, with lemon wedges for squeezing over.

Steak for Two

Everyone has their favourite cut of steak and the way they like it cooked. I go for a bavette or onglet medium-rare - but choose what you like best. For ease as much as presentation, I buy a large steak for 2 people and serve it sliced. Just keep your pan super-hot, be mindful of timing, go heavy on the salt and pepper, and once it's basted in butter, it'll be just as good as one from a steakhouse. Start by taking your steak out of the fridge an hour before cooking to let it come to room temperature; this is when you can also start to make the chips.

400g (1lb) your favourite cut of steak, about 2.5cm (1in) thick

1 tbsp olive oil

1 tbsp salted butter

1 small bunch of whatever woody herbs you fancy, such as rosemary, thyme or sage

sea salt and freshly ground black pepper

Take the steak out of the fridge and remove any packaging 1 hour before you want to cook it. Pat the steak dry and season both sides with plenty of salt and pepper - you want lots so don't be shy. When you're ready to start cooking, drizzle the steak with the olive oil and make sure it's completely coated.

Heat the frying pan on a very high heat until smoking hot. Place the steak in the pan and once it hits the heat, don't touch - you want it to form a crust before you even think about turning. Cook to your liking following the timings below:

Rare: 2 minutes on each side
Medium-rare: 3½ minutes on each side
Medium: 4½ minutes on each side
Well done: 5-6 minutes on each side

In the last minute of cooking the steak on its second side, add the butter and herbs. Baste the steak with the herby butter for another minute, then remove from the pan. Leave to rest for 10 minutes. Slice and serve with your choice of sauce, chips, and gratin.

A Choice of Sauces

Deciding between these two sauces is my greatest dilemma every time I read a restaurant menu when I'm ordering a steak. I'm now making you choose, but you can't go wrong with either option.

BÉARNAISE SAUCE

1 small bunch of tarragon

½ shallot, very finely chopped, about 1 tbsp

1 tsp black peppercorns, crushed

2 tbsp white wine vinegar

2 egg yolks

100g (½ cup minus 1 tbsp) cold unsalted butter,
cut into small cubes

a generous pinch of salt

a splash of lemon juice

Separate the tarragon leaves from the stalks. Finely
chop 1 tablespoon of the leaves and set aside. Use
something heavy, like the end of a rolling pin,
to bruise the tarragon stalks and add them to a small
pan with the shallot, crushed peppercorns and
vinegar. Bring to a simmer over a very low heat
and let the vinegar reduce by half.

Pour the vinegar mixture through a sieve into
a heatproof bowl set over a pan of simmering water.
Don't let the water touch the bottom of the bowl.
Stirring with a balloon whisk, add the egg yolks and
as you feel the yolks start to thicken, add the butter,
a cube at a time, until combined. Have a few cubes
of ice to hand just in case the sauce starts to split.
If it does split, throw in an ice cube and the sauce
should settle with some stirring. Once all the butter
has been added and the sauce is thick and golden,
take it off the heat. Stir through the reserved tarragon
and season with salt and lemon juice to taste.

PEPPERCORN SAUCE

1 tsp whole black peppercorns

1 tsp green peppercorns in brine, drained

½ small shallot, very finely diced

20ml (1¼ tbsp) cognac

100ml (6½ tbsp) double (heavy) cream

a splash of Worcestershire sauce

½ tsp salted butter

In either a pestle and mortar or mini food processor,
grind the black and green peppercorns together
until coarsely ground, but not too fine.

While the steak is resting, add the shallot to the
leftover fat in the pan used to cook the steak and
turn the heat to medium-high. Fry the shallot until
softened, then stir in the crushed peppercorns and
cook for a few minutes until fragrant.

Turn up the heat, pour in the cognac and tilt the
pan or use a match to set the sauce alight. Once
the flame dissipates, pour in the cream and splash
of Worcestershire sauce. Turn the heat down and
let the sauce simmer for 2–3 minutes, until reduced.
Add the butter and any juices left over from the
steak after resting. Serve the sauce with the steak.

Joe's Chips With Tarragon Salt

When my boyfriend Joe and I met, one of the first
questions I asked him was naturally, "What do you
like to cook?" He said something about fried rice
and fish fingers but ended with "…but I really
do make the world's best chips". Five years later
and this is still true. No matter what I do, time
after time, his chips outdo mine. This is his
method that he's perfected in our kitchen.

2–3 large floury potatoes, about 500g (1lb 2oz)
in total, left unpeeled and sliced into thick
French fries

a generous drizzle of olive oil

2 tbsp sea salt, plus extra to season

1 tbsp tarragon leaves

freshly ground black pepper

Heat the oven to 180°C fan (400°F/Gas 6).

Put a large pot of salty water on to boil. Add the
chips to the boiling water and cook for 10 minutes,
then drain. Put the potatoes back in the empty
pot to steam dry and give them a shake.

Place the chips on a large baking tray and leave
to cool for 10 minutes. Pour a generous drizzle
of olive oil over the chips, season with a little
salt and lots of pepper and bake for 30 minutes.
Halfway through, take the tray out of the oven
and leave the chips to cool for 10 minutes before
popping them back into the oven for a final
15 minutes.

While the chips are baking, make the tarragon
salt. Crush the salt with the tarragon either in
a pestle and mortar or a mini food processor
until combined, and the salt turns deep green
in colour.

As soon as the chips are done and super crisp,
sprinkle over some of the tarragon salt to taste.

Serve the chips with the steak and your choice
of sauce. Keep any remaining tarragon salt
in an airtight jar and use on eggs, sprinkled
over a tomato salad or on a piece of grilled fish.

Creamed Spinach Gratin

A side dish can sometimes feel just as exciting as the steak and this is one of those, deserving more love than it sometimes gets.

150ml (⅔ cup) double (heavy) cream

¼ white onion or ½ shallot, finely diced

1 bay leaf

1 clove

a pinch of freshly grated nutmeg

¼ tsp freshly ground black pepper

½ tsp sea salt

2 tbsp finely grated Parmesan cheese, plus extra to serve (or you can use Gruyère)

2 garlic cloves, finely grated

250g (9oz) chopped frozen spinach, defrosted

2 tbsp panko breadcrumbs

Heat the oven to 180°C fan (400°F/Gas 6).

Pour the cream into a small pan, add the onion or shallot, bay leaf and clove, then simmer over a medium-low heat for 10 minutes to infuse. Remove the bay and clove. Stir in the nutmeg, pepper, salt, half of the Parmesan and the garlic and turn the heat to low.

Squeeze out any excess liquid from the spinach, then stir it into the pan. Tip the spinach mixture into a small gratin dish. Mix the rest of the Parmesan with the breadcrumbs and sprinkle over the top.

Bake for 35–40 minutes, until the top is crisp and golden. Serve with the steak and chips.

Crêpes Suzette

My brother, Conor, is the king of crêpes Suzette and adheres to the principle that you only need to master one perfect dessert and your friends and family will forever request it. The Campari in the sauce brings a note of a Negroni and helps to cut through the caramel. The crêpes can be made in advance along with the sauce, then kept in the fridge until needed. I usually serve 2–3 pancakes each, and this batter makes a few extra just in case any fail (or for the cook to snack on).

140g (1 cup) plain (all-purpose) flour

1 heaped tbsp caster (superfine) sugar

a pinch of sea salt

2 eggs

340ml (1½ cups minus 2 tsp) whole milk

4 tsp unsalted butter, melted and left to cool, plus extra for cooking the pancakes

scoops of vanilla ice cream, to serve

CAMPARI AND ORANGE SAUCE

2 tbsp Grand Marnier, plus extra to serve

1 tbsp Campari

200ml (scant 1 cup) fresh orange juice

1 tsp finely grated unwaxed orange zest

2 tbsp caster (superfine) sugar

2 oranges, peeled, segmented or sliced

1 tbsp (15g) cold unsalted butter

First make the pancake batter. In a mixing bowl, mix the flour, sugar and salt. Add the eggs, milk and melted butter. Stir until smooth and let sit for 1 hour.

Melt a little butter in a large, non-stick frying pan and turn the heat to high. When the pan is hot, pour 75ml (5 tablespoons) of the batter into the pan, then tilt the pan to spread the batter out thinly. Cook for 1 minute, until the base is golden. Flip the pancake and cook the other side for 30 seconds. Fold the crêpe in half, then in half again. Repeat to cook 4–6 pancakes for 2 people, adding more butter as needed. Set aside while you make the sauce.

In a small bowl, mix the Grand Marnier, Campari, orange juice and orange zest and set to one side.

Start with the pan off the heat and sprinkle in an even layer of sugar to cover the base. Turn the heat to medium, put the pan on the heat and let the sugar caramelize without stirring; it should take a few minutes to melt. Stir in the Grand Marnier mix, then turn down the heat and cook for a few minutes until reduced. Stir in the oranges and butter then, when melted, add the folded crêpes. Spoon the sauce over the crêpes and simmer for a few minutes to allow them to absorb the sauce.

Serve the crêpes with extra Grand Marnier poured over and set alight, if you fancy, along with scoops of vanilla ice cream.

Apple Pie à la Mode

This is not your classic apple pie and really is more of a galette in form, but it encompasses all the elements that I love most about a proper pie. The slightly sharp green apples are coated in a salted caramel that's spiced with cinnamon and nutmeg and scented with a little lemon zest, then encased in a rich soured cream pastry. Both the pastry and filling can be made the day before serving and simply assembled just before baking. Serve the pie warm à la mode, in other words with big scoops of vanilla ice cream on top.

100g (¾ cup) plain (all-purpose) flour

25g (scant ¼ cup) icing (confectioners') sugar

a pinch of sea salt

50g (3½ tbsp) cold salted butter, cut into small pieces

25ml (1½ tbsp) soured cream

1 egg

½ tbsp granulated sugar

scoops of vanilla ice cream, to serve

CARAMEL APPLE FILLING

25g (scant ¼ cup) caster (superfine) sugar

1½ tbsp double (heavy) cream

a pinch of sea salt

a pinch of freshly ground nutmeg

¼ tsp ground cinnamon

¼ tsp cornflour (cornstarch)

¼ tsp finely grated unwaxed lemon zest

2 Granny Smith apples, peeled, cored and each cut into 8 slices

First make the soured cream pastry. Sift the flour, icing sugar and salt together in a large mixing bowl. Add the butter and rub in with your fingers until the mixture resembles fine breadcrumbs. Add the soured cream and stir in with a fork and then your hands to make a smooth ball of dough. Wrap the dough and place in the fridge to chill for a few hours or overnight.

To make the filling, add the sugar and 2 teaspoons water to a sauté pan and turn the heat to medium-high. Watch the mixture, but don't stir it, and just when it turns a deep honey-brown, pour in the cream and turn the heat down to low. Add the salt, spices, cornflour and lemon zest and stir gently together. Add the apples, making sure they're coated in the caramel as you stir. Simmer the apples for 10 minutes, until softened on the outside but still firm in the middle, and they hold their shape. Turn the heat off and let cool in the pan before transferring to a dish and chilling in the fridge.

Heat the oven to 180°C fan (400°F/Gas 6) and line a large baking tray with baking (parchment) paper.

To assemble the pie, roll out the pastry between 2 sheets of baking paper into a large circle, about 25cm (10in) in diameter and 4mm (¼in) thick. Place the pastry on the prepared baking tray and spoon the apple filling in the middle. Roughly fold the edge of the pastry about a quarter of the way over the filling, pleating it where needed, to make a round, free-form pie.

Whisk the egg with a splash of water and, using a pastry brush, paint the edge of the pastry, then sprinkle with the granulated sugar. Bake the pie for 45 minutes, until the pastry is golden and cooked through. Let sit for a few minutes, then serve warm with scoops of vanilla ice cream.

The Thousand-Layer Heart With Rhubarb and Cardamom Custard

Celebrate love: celebrate the kitsch, the cringe and the complexities of it all with a heart-shaped dessert that you'll want to share with someone you love. The first time I made this was for a friend who was spending her first Valentine's Day single after a big breakup. I wanted to make her feel better with something special. The crisp, light layers of pastry are sandwiched with a creamy, cardamom-spiced custard with pieces of bright-pink rhubarb to cut through the sweetness. Inspired by my favourite thing to order at any French pâtisserie, mille-feuille, which translates to "a thousand leaves", my thousand-layer heart is heavenly and hopefully on the good side of kitsch.

PASTRY HEARTS

1 egg

1 tsp icing (confectioners') sugar, plus extra for dusting

plain (all-purpose) flour, for dusting

1 ready-rolled sheet of all-butter puff pastry, about 350g (12oz)

BAKED RHUBARB

3 rhubarb stalks, chopped into 2.5cm (1in) pieces

1 tsp caster (superfine) sugar

¼ tsp finely grated zest and juice of 1 unwaxed orange

CARDAMOM CUSTARD

250ml (1 cup plus 1 tbsp) whole milk

3 cardamom pods, crushed

2 egg yolks

45g (¼ cup) caster (superfine) sugar

1 tbsp cornflour (cornstarch)

½ tsp vanilla paste

Start by roasting the rhubarb. Heat the oven to 180°C fan (400°F/Gas 6) and place the rhubarb in a baking dish. Sprinkle over the sugar, orange zest and juice. Roast for 15 minutes, until tender but it still holds its shape. Set aside to cool completely while you make the pastry hearts.

Turn the oven up to 200°C fan (425°F/Gas 7) and line 2 baking trays with baking (parchment) paper. Whisk together the egg and icing sugar to make an egg wash and set aside.

Lightly dust the work surface with flour and roll out the pastry with a rolling pin into a long rectangular shape, about half the width of the original sheet and 4mm (¼in) thick. Draw a heart shape, roughly 15cm (6in) in diameter, on a piece of paper and cut it out. Lay the paper down on the pastry and use a knife to cut around the paper to make a heart shape, then repeat to cut out a second heart shape. Roll the remaining pastry out again, if needed, to cut a third heart. Place the hearts on the lined trays and brush over the egg wash. Bake for 15 minutes, until golden and crisp. Remove the top layer from two of the hearts to make a flat base for filling. Leave to cool on a rack.

While the pastry hearts are baking, make the cardamom custard. In a pan, simmer the milk and cardamom pods on a low heat for 10 minutes. Whisk together the egg yolks and caster sugar in a mixing bowl until pale and creamy. Add the cornflour and whisk again.

Strain the warm milk, discard the cardamom, and slowly add to the egg mixture, whisking continuously. Return to the pan and on a very low heat and whisk for 15 minutes, until the custard thickens to the consistency of thick Greek yogurt. Stir in the vanilla and let cool. Once cool, put in the freezer for a few hours to chill completely.

Assemble just before serving. Place one trimmed pastry heart on a plate and spoon over 4 tablespoons of the custard, then spread out evenly. Spoon over half of the rhubarb and syrup, then place the second trimmed pastry heart on top. Repeat with another layer of custard and rhubarb, finishing with the third pastry heart. Dust the top with icing sugar.

Vanilla Milkshake Cake With Roasted Strawberries and Cream

This is "summer in a cake" and is best made when strawberries are sweet and in season. The method is inspired by *tres leches* cakes, as the vanilla milkshake mix is poured over the top of the warm sponge, then chilled until served. The malted milk powder gives an incredible depth of flavour, yet the cake remains light enough to make you feel it's never too much, even after a second or third slice.

VANILLA MILKSHAKE CAKE

2 eggs, separated

a pinch of salt

100g (½ cup plus 1 tbsp) caster (superfine) sugar

3 tsp vanilla paste or extract

100ml (6½ tbsp) buttermilk

100g (¾ cup) plain (all-purpose) flour

½ tsp baking powder

½ tsp bicarbonate of soda (baking soda)

100ml (6½ tbsp) whole milk

1 tsp icing (confectioners') sugar

2 tsp malted milk powder

1 tbsp soured cream or crème fraîche

ROASTED STRAWBERRIES AND WHIPPED CREAM

300g (10oz) strawberries, hulled and halved

1 tsp caster (superfine) sugar

a drop of rosewater

200ml (scant 1 cup) double (heavy) cream

¼ tsp icing (confectioners') sugar

Heat the oven to 180°C fan (400°F/Gas 6). Line the base and sides of a 15cm (6in) square cake tin with baking (parchment) paper.

First roast the strawberries. Place them, cut-side down, in a baking dish, and sprinkle with the caster sugar and rosewater. Roast for 20 minutes, until soft but they still hold their shape. Set aside (you can keep them in the fridge if leaving the cake to cool overnight).

While the strawberries are roasting, whisk the egg whites with the salt in a clean, grease-free mixing bowl using an electric hand whisk until they start to form stiff peaks. Slowly add the caster sugar, about a third at a time, and continue to whisk until glossy, firm peaks.

In a separate mixing bowl, whisk the egg yolks, 2 teaspoons of the vanilla and buttermilk until smooth.

Sift the flour, baking powder and bicarbonate of soda together in a separate bowl and add to the egg yolk mix, a third at a time, slowly folding everything together. Don't worry if the mixture looks quite thick and lumpy – it will all come together. Gently fold in the whipped egg whites, a third at a time, until combined – don't overmix; it should be light and airy.

Spoon the cake mixture into the lined tin and level the top. Bake for 35 minutes, until light golden, risen, and a skewer inserted into the middle comes out clean. Leave the cake to cool in the tin for 10 minutes, then use a skewer to poke holes in the top of the cake.

As the cake is cooling, whisk the milk with the icing sugar, malted milk powder, remaining vanilla and soured cream or crème fraîche until smooth. Spoon the mixture evenly over the top of the cake, then leave to cool completely. When cool, cover the cake tin and chill for at least 4 hours or overnight.

Just before serving, lightly whip the cream with the icing sugar in a large mixing bowl until soft peaks form.

To serve, remove the cake from the tin and peel off the lining paper. Spoon the whipped cream over the cake and top with the roasted strawberries.

Risking Tiers
on Chocolate Cake

When I was 16, I fell completely and utterly in love with my high-school crush. After a year of talking about films and music online and ignoring each other in the hallways between classes, we finally went on a date. He kissed me at the bus stop after an afternoon eating mint-choc-chip ice cream down by Sydney harbour, and I felt like I had everything that I could ever wish for. We met up after school from then on every day, sharing headphones to listen to albums we liked and $1 char sui buns from the Chinese grocer under the train station, until we had to tear ourselves away from each other and go home to opposite sides of the city.

A few months in, my parents went away for a week and although my grandparents were looking after my brother and me at night, the house was empty during the day. This week fell on our school's annual sports carnival, a day I usually feigned some sort of injury and spent at home sitting on the sofa. I called in sick and so did my boyfriend; we were going to have a grown-up day to ourselves we decided. I wanted to make a proper occasion of it, and this required a cake I thought. I'd never cooked or made anything for him before, but I desperately wanted to impress so I turned to the woman whose recipes still answer issues of this sort to this day: Nigella. I woke up fizzing with nerves and got to work on her recipe for Sour Cream Chocolate Cake.

Annoyingly, I left the cake in the oven for too long as I was curling my hair and applying probably my tenth layer of mascara, and the edges of the cake were black and as crisp as my eyelashes when I took it out of the oven. So, using a bowl as a template, I cut out small rounds from each of the cakes and prayed the icing would hide it all. A tub of soured cream, butter, melted dark chocolate and golden syrup were whipped until light and fluffy; it was going to be perfect I thought.

My boyfriend was due to arrive any minute so even though the cakes were still a little warm, I covered them with icing and assembled the layers of sponge. One layer of cake was okay, then the second, but by the time the third layer was ready to be placed on top, everything started to slide. More icing I thought was the answer and the tall three-tier cake was leaning like the Tower of Pisa by the time the doorbell rang. It held on long enough for him to see it before the whole thing collapsed onto the kitchen bench in a gooey mess.

Nevertheless, we ate huge slices of the cake, in near silence as it was the first time we'd been properly alone together somewhere private; chocolate cake will always remind me of times of tender teenage awkwardness. It didn't matter the cake fell apart: all I cared about was that it was a Wednesday; we were eating cake for lunch; and we were going to spend the afternoon together laying in the sunshine down by the rock pools in the bay beneath my house. He didn't turn out to be the love of my life that I thought he was at 16, but we were together for 4 years until I was 20, and by the time we broke up, I had learnt a lot from mistakes in both love and the kitchen. I don't regret risking that extra tier or two on the chocolate cake or anything else; love like cooking is for making mistakes.

That cake was the first proper thing I had cooked by myself, start to finish. Even though my heart still sinks as I think about watching the layers of melted icing drip from the still-warm sponge, it reminds me of what it was like to be young and have a whole life of adventures ahead, in both cooking and love. I was just 18 when I left my Mum's kitchen and started to cook on my own. In those first few years, there were a lot of disasters. It felt like fire alarms didn't stop going off, there

"Life is short, make those traditions, take risks, cook for people you care for, and please always let cakes cool before you ice them."

were numerous ovens full of smoke, tears over split custard, and ingredients I couldn't make sense of. Each was a blessing though because it taught me that trying again is the only way to get better.

Sure, cooking for someone you love is a "language of love", but it's also a way of showing someone that you really see them. When words don't quite work, when you want to make someone feel like everything will be okay, when you want to show someone that their joy is your joy, you can cook. The time that we spend at the table throughout our lives celebrating, crying, laughing and kissing is what keeps us going.

I remember every occasion where someone I love went out of their way to make me something special: the pumpkin soup with lots of nutmeg that my Granny had simmering on the stove every time I went over, that she lovingly served with swirls of cream and ribbons of basil; the banana smoothies

with oats, and everything else in the cupboard, that Dad would blend for our breakfast when he was home on the weekend; and the traybake Joe makes with crispy chorizo, potatoes and peppers that he's perfected by tucking in a bay leaf and adding extra chillies, just how I like it. To cook someone food they love, despite the effort, is love in action.

Find the dishes you make to remember what it felt like when you first fell in love, the ones you prepare for your 5th, 10th and 15th anniversary, with the muscle memory of how to cook them imprinted on your hands. Make desserts that appear once the tablecloth is already stained with three different bottles of wine (and maybe a Campari or two). These are recipes that call for candles to celebrate everything from the big to the small. Life is short, make those traditions, take risks, cook for people you care for, and please always let cakes cool before you ice them.

Collapsing Chocolate Cake

This cake is a thing of beauty, despite all its broken parts. Its name comes from the moment you remove it from the oven, then drop it – on purpose – to cause the middle of the cake to collapse in on itself. This cake is flourless and made super light by folding the whisked egg whites through the batter, which means its both crunchy and soft, much like meringue. Complete with crisp edges, an almost custard-like middle and just enough coffee and vanilla to bring out the notes of the dark chocolate, it's the cake of my dreams. Make sure to bake it on a low shelf in your oven, as this baby blooms like a soufflé when it cooks, so it needs space to rise. You can serve it plain, but I love filling the middle with whipped cream and fresh berries.

150g (1¼ sticks) salted butter, cut into pieces, plus extra for greasing

250g (9oz) 70% plain (semisweet) chocolate, broken into pieces

1 tsp vanilla extract

120ml (½ cup) strong cold coffee

220g (1 cup plus 3 tbsp) caster (superfine) sugar

a pinch of sea salt

4 eggs, separated

200ml (scant 1 cup) double (heavy) cream

1 tsp icing (confectioners') sugar, plus extra for dusting

a mix of fresh fruit, such as raspberries, blackberries and cherries, to decorate

Heat the oven to 160°C fan (350°F/Gas 4). Line the base and sides of a 16cm (6½in) springform cake tin with baking (parchment) paper. The paper should sit above the sides of the tin; use the leftover butter on the wrapper to help stick it.

Melt the butter and chocolate together in a double boiler or heatproof bowl set over a pan of gently simmering water, stir to combine, then pour into a large mixing bowl. Stir in the vanilla, coffee, sugar and salt. Let the mixture cool for 10 minutes or so; don't worry if it looks split – I promise it's all good.

As the chocolate mixture cools, whisk the egg whites in a clean, grease-free mixing bowl with an electric hand whisk until they form stiff peaks. Set aside.

Using the same electric whisk, mix the egg yolks into the melted chocolate, one at a time, until the mixture looks like a thick custard. Spoon one-third of the egg whites into the chocolate and briefly blitz with the electric whisk to loosen the mix. Fold in the rest of the egg whites with a metal spoon, keeping as much lightness and air in the cake batter as possible.

Gently tip the cake batter into the lined springform tin and bake on a low shelf for 40 minutes, until risen like a soufflé; the centre will be soft and gooey, but the sides should be crisp.

Now, this next step may go against all reasoning: take the cake out of the oven, lift it in its tin then drop from a 5cm (2in) height onto your work counter. This will force the middle of the cake to collapse evenly as it cools and create the perfect bowl-like shape for the whipped cream and berries. Leave the cake to cool completely in the tin, then chill for a firmer, fudge-like texture or keep at room temperature for a gooey, soft inside.

When you're ready to serve, whip the cream with the icing sugar until light and fluffy. Spoon the whipped cream into the middle of the cake, pile the berries and cherries on top and dust with a little extra icing sugar, if you like.

The Most Perfect Pavlova

To me, a plate of pavlova is pure joy. It's the balance of crisp meringue, the wobble of the marshmallow centre, the cold cream and tart fruit, which cuts through the richness, to make it one of the world's best desserts. I especially love the flavour and the look of passionfruit, with its bright yellow pulp and black seeds, in contrast to the paleness of the whipped cream.

As an Australian, I have strict requirements on what makes a pavlova perfect: all too often I've seen them fall short, but a sure-fire way to make sure that doesn't happen is to focus on the egg whites. Both the beaters and the mixing bowl you use must be thoroughly wiped down with white wine or cider vinegar or lemon juice to ensure there's no grease-like residue, as this will interfere with the egg whites becoming light and cloud-like. This recipe is based on Australian cook and restaurateur, Stephanie Alexander's classic pavlova, which is failsafe, and involves flipping the meringue over once baked so the cream filling doesn't soften the crisp edges of the meringue.

3 egg whites, at room temperature

a pinch of sea salt

200g (1 cup) golden caster (superfine) sugar

1 heaped tsp cornflour (cornstarch)

½ tsp white wine or cider vinegar

1 tsp vanilla paste or extract

100ml (6½ tbsp) double (heavy) cream

4 tbsp Greek yogurt

5 passionfruit, cut in half and pulp scooped out

Heat the oven to 180°C fan (400°F/Gas 6). Line a baking tray with baking (parchment) paper.

In a large, clean, grease-free mixing bowl, whisk the egg whites with the salt using an electric hand whisk until they start to form stiff peaks. Slowly add the sugar, little by little, until the meringue forms stiff shiny peaks. Sprinkle over the cornflour, vinegar and vanilla and fold in lightly with a metal spoon.

Spoon the meringue onto the lined baking tray in one large pile, making sure you retain the air. Smooth out the edges to form a circular shape, about 20cm (8in) in diameter, with a flattened top. When you're happy with the shape, gently place the meringue in the oven.

Turn the oven down to 140°C fan (325°F/Gas 3) and bake for 30 minutes, then reduce the temperature further to 120°C fan (275°F/Gas 1) and cook for another 40 minutes. Turn off the heat and leave the pavlova to cool in the oven with the door left slightly ajar, propped open with a folded tea towel, if necessary.

When you're ready to serve, lightly whip the cream in a large bowl with an electric hand whisk, then gently fold in the yogurt.

Take the pavlova out of the cool oven and carefully turn it upside down on a serving plate so that the crisp, crunchy top is now on the bottom and the flat marshmallowy base is on top. Spoon over the cream mix and top with the passionfruit pulp. Serve the pavlova straight away, returning to the leftovers the next day for the best breakfast ever.

OTHER FRUIT TOPPINGS

You can try any fruit you fancy to top your perfect pavlova, but I think that using a type that isn't too sweet is key. Try raspberries, gooseberries or kiwi fruit for the best in both colour and flavour.

Banana Fritters With Drunk Chocolate Sauce

"Banana fritters with chocolate sauce and ice cream, it was what we ate on one of our first dates at the drive-through cinema," said my Nan, Judy, to me the last time I ever saw her. She was reminiscing about her romance with my grandfather, Barry, who had passed away a few years earlier. Sixty years after she first ate them, it was something that still made her smile. We spoke about all the recipes I wanted to write for this book, and I promised I'd make her the best version of banana fritters to celebrate that moment of sharing them with her first and only love.

I'm a result of that romance and have inherited her love of all things fried and dusted with icing sugar. These banana fritters are hard not to smile about; they have a super-crisp batter and come with a thick, rum-infused chocolate sauce drizzled over the top and a scoop of ice cream. I like to use a heavy, cast-iron pot when I'm deep frying as it retains an even, consistent heat as the fritters become gorgeous and golden.

BANANA FRITTERS

300ml (1¼ cups) flavourless oil, such as sunflower or canola (rapeseed)

130g (1 cup) plain (all-purpose) flour, plus extra for dusting

½ tsp baking powder

a pinch of sea salt

200ml (scant 1 cup) ice-cold fizzy water

2 just-ripe bananas, halved lengthways, then peeled

icing (confectioners') sugar, to dust

a few scoops of vanilla ice cream, to serve

DRUNK CHOCOLATE SAUCE

90g (3¼oz) 70% plain (semisweet) chocolate, broken into pieces

120ml (½ cup) double (heavy) cream

a pinch of sea salt

a shot of dark rum

Start by making the drunk chocolate sauce. Melt the chocolate with the cream, salt and rum either in a double boiler or in a heatproof bowl set over a pan of gently simmering water, then stir until smooth. (You can make the sauce in advance of serving, then gently heat it again when ready.)

To make the banana fritters, first heat the oil in a large, deep, heavy-based saucepan or deep-fat fryer until 180°C (350°F), or until a pinch of flour sizzles on the surface.

While the oil is heating, make the batter by whisking together the flour, baking powder, salt and fizzy water in a mixing bowl until smooth.

Dust the banana halves in a little extra flour, then dip into the batter until coated all over and place straight into the hot oil. Fry the bananas in 2 batches for 3–4 minutes, turning halfway, until golden and crisp. Using a slotted spoon, transfer the banana fritters to a kitchen paper-lined plate to drain, and fry the remaining bananas.

Arrange the banana fritters on 2 plates, dust with icing sugar and serve drizzled with the drunk chocolate sauce and a scoop of ice cream. Save any bits of fried batter to scatter over too, while extra sauce can be served in a jug (jar) on the side.

Fig Leaf and White Peach Parfait

Fig leaves have an aroma of almonds – they're the scent you breathe in when you walk past a fig tree on a hot day – and taste like a combination of vanilla and coconut. I have been known to make Mum stop her car at the side of the road after spotting a fig tree, just so I could grab a few leaves, and I once made this dessert with a few leaves from a fig tree facing the Colosseum in Rome. The night I made this dessert in my tiny yellow kitchen in a rental flat next to Campo de' Fiori market in Rome, I could hardly wait the 5 hours needed for the parfait to properly chill and kept dipping a spoon in to "taste test". I use David Lebovitz's method of toasting the fig leaves to intensify the flavour in the custard, which will make your home smell like a holiday.

3-4 small fig leaves or 1 large leaf

250ml (1 cup plus 1 tbsp) whole milk

1 egg

1½ tbsp caster (superfine) sugar

1 tsp vanilla paste or extract

3½ tbsp amaretto, sherry or vin santo

85-100g (3-3½oz) savoiardi biscuits (ladyfingers), about 8-10 in total

2 ripe white peaches, sliced

100ml (6½ tbsp) double (heavy) cream

1½ tbsp icing (confectioners') sugar, sifted

200g (7oz) sesame snaps

APRICOTS AND ALMONDS

Instead of peaches, roast 200g (7oz) apricots in a 180°C fan (400°F/Gas 6) oven with a sprinkle of sugar and strip of lemon peel for 25 minutes, until soft. Leave to cool, then cut the apricots in half, remove the stones and slice. Stir 1 teaspoon almond extract into the custard. Assemble as instructed, right, but top with toasted flaked almonds instead of sesame snaps.

In a dry, heavy-bottomed pot, lightly toast the fig leaves on both sides on a medium-high heat until fragrant; a little hiss and sizzle is fine – they'll soften slightly with the heat and start scenting your kitchen. When the leaves have wilted, pour the milk over, then turn the heat to very low and simmer for 10-15 minutes, until the fig leaves infuse and scent the milk.

Meanwhile, whisk the egg, caster sugar and vanilla in a large mixing bowl until pale and creamy. Using a ladle, scoop out a little of the warm milk and add it to the eggs and quickly whisk it in.

Strain the rest of the milk through a sieve into the mixing bowl and discard the fig leaves, stir to combine, then return the mixture to the pan. Turn the heat to medium-low and stir continuously with a wooden spoon until the mixture thickens enough to coat the back of the spoon. Take the pan off the heat and leave to one side to cool, then transfer to a bowl and chill for about 2 hours, until thickened.

To assemble the parfait, spoon about half of the custard in the bottom of 2 tall parfait glasses (you can also use a glass dish).

Pour your liquor of choice into a shallow bowl, then dunk in a savoiardi biscuit (ladyfinger) and place in one of the glasses on top of the custard. Repeat until you've created an even layer of liquor-soaked biscuits in both glasses. Cover the biscuits with half of the remaining custard and top with half of the peaches. Spoon over the rest of the custard, cover each glass and chill for at least 5 hours to allow the flavours to mingle.

When you're ready to serve, cover the top with a layer of the remaining peaches. Lightly whip the cream and icing sugar in a large mixing bowl with an electric hand whisk until soft peaks, then spoon the cream over the peaches. Smash the sesame snaps into a mixture of small pieces and larger shards and sprinkle over the top of the parfaits, then serve.

Mango and Vanilla Cream Cloud Cake

This is probably my most favourite cake in the whole world – it's literally light as a feather and soft as I imagine a cloud would be. It's an incredibly adaptable cake too – you can fill it with whatever you fancy, although when mangoes are in season and at their best, I can't resist pairing them with the lightly whipped vanilla-cream filling, sandwiched between the sponge layers. Inspired by Hong Kong mango pancakes – which I would patiently wait for at the end of every weekend dim-sum lunch at Chinese restaurants across Sydney and Singapore – the secret to the success of this cake is to whip the egg whites well, as you slowly add the sugar, as well as the egg yolks. The flour is then folded in gently, so you don't lose any precious air.

CLOUD CAKE

20g (1½ tbsp) unsalted butter, plus extra for greasing

1 tsp vanilla extract

3 large eggs, separated

a pinch of salt

120g (1 cup) caster (superfine) sugar

90g (¾ cup) plain (all-purpose) flour, plus extra for dusting

½ tsp baking powder

MANGO AND VANILLA CREAM

150ml (⅔ cup) whipping cream

2 tbsp kefir or Greek yogurt

1 heaped tsp icing (confectioners') sugar

½ tsp vanilla paste

1 ripe mango, peeled, stone removed and sliced

edible flowers, such as pansies and violas, to decorate (optional)

Heat the oven to 180°C fan (400°F/Gas 6). Line a 15cm (6in) springform cake tin with baking (parchment) paper and butter and flour the sides.

Melt the butter with the vanilla and 2 tablespoons water in a small pan over a low heat and leave to cool slightly.

In a large, clean, grease-free mixing bowl, whisk the egg whites with the salt using an electric hand whisk until they form stiff peaks. Slowly add the sugar, little by little, until you have a smooth, glossy meringue. Add the egg yolks, one at a time, whisking well between each addition. Whisk for a further 2 minutes, until you have a light, pale mixture.

Sift the flour and baking powder into a separate bowl. Gently fold the flour mix into the egg mix with a large metal spoon, taking care not to lose too much air.

Slowly fold the melted butter mix into the cake batter, a little at a time, until combined.

Pour the cake batter into the tin. Bake for 30 minutes, until well risen and golden on top, and starting to come away from the sides of the tin. Leave the cake to cool in the tin. While the cake is cooling, drape a clean kitchen towel over the top to prevent it from drying out.

Meanwhile, make the mango and vanilla cream. In a large mixing bowl, whip the cream, kefir or yogurt, icing sugar and vanilla until they form soft peaks – you don't want it too stiff, just softly whipped. Chill the whipped cream until ready to serve.

Once the cake has completely cooled, use a bread knife to slice it in half through the middle. Place one sponge on a serving plate and spoon over half of the whipped cream. Top with the sliced mango. Place the second sponge on top, then spoon over the remaining cream and decorate with edible flowers, if you fancy.

Acknowledgments

I can't quite believe that what I'm sitting here writing is the acknowledgment to my own cookbook. It's surreal to say the least and is a privilege that's only possible because of the support, love and trust of so many people.

To Stephanie Milner and Katie Cowan, without you, I would not be on my balcony writing acknowledgements for a book with my name on it. Thank you for believing in me. To Nicola Graimes for her constant support over the months of editing this book. To Tania Da Silva Gomes for being there through the design process and for patiently listening to me try to explain the moods of different fonts. To Lucy Sienkowska for holding my hand through the writing of this book, you made what could be chaotic so calm. To the entire DK marketing and press teams including Fran Gizauskas and Cora Siedlecka.

Seeing this book come to life at Narroway Studios was so special and such a joy. Thank you to Issy Croker for your magic behind the camera, soundtrack skills and calico cat chat. To Emily Ezekiel, you are a pasta twirling genius, the creator of the best-looking roast chicken I've ever eaten and my dream prop shopper. Thank you to Matilda Goad, Tekla Fabrics, Grace Floral London and Helle Mardahl for sending such lovely things for these pages. To Ozuola Martins for counsel on all things fashion. To Hugo Harrison, Clare Cole, Egle Loit, and Lucy Rose Turnbull for all of your help on the shoot. Thank you to everyone at Evi-O. Studio, even before this book had a title, you were my dream designer to turn it into a reality.

To every single reader of my weekly newsletter, *Dishes To Delight*, I can't imagine a Sunday night not writing to you all and without you, this book might not have been born. To the chefs, restaurants, and cities written about throughout this book that inspire me every time I step into the kitchen, thank you for feeding my desire to cook and eat. To friends like Holly Temple, Georgia Rudd, Ana Kinsella, Tahmina Begum, Jordan Turner, Rosalind Jana, Sharlene Teo, and Rhiannon Lucy Cosslett for being there with advice that's worth its weight in gold. To the whole team at Courier, especially Ben Chiou and Danny Giacopelli.

A special thank you to Rachel Khoo, Otegha Uwagba, Natasha Lunn, Ravneet Gill, Laura Goodman, Rachel Roddy, and Anna Sulan Masing, your words of wisdom throughout my career have let me find a place to cook and write in the world. To Kate Evans, my agent and the person who completely changed my life over breakfast back in 2019. Your unwavering support has been a solace that has sustained me through it all.

This book is a love letter to the four people I love to cook for most, my best friend Maddi, my boyfriend Joe and my Mum and Dad. Maddi, you are truly my sunlight when things are feeling grey and have always been by my side no matter the distance. There's no one I'd rather drink cheap wine in the sunshine with. Joe, no words would be enough to thank you. Simply put this book wouldn't exist without you. You were my *Table for Two* companion throughout every single one of these recipes, washed every dish, made every cup of tea, poured every glass of wine and read every single word as soon as it was written throughout the process of working on it. You have my whole heart. Dad, for showing me that words hold beauty and power beyond what we know. Mum for teaching me everything I know about food and about love, you taught me to have an appetite for everything.

About the Author

Bre Graham is an Australian writer and editor. Published in *Refinery 29*, *The Guardian*, *Riposte*, *Harper's Bazaar*, *Timeout*, *NY Mag*, and many more, she is currently the Lifestyle Editor at Courier Media. Bre regularly hosts podcasts, panels and supper clubs, and writes the hit newsletter *Dishes to Delight* on the joy of cooking and love. She lives in London and spends almost all her time contemplating her next meal.

@breaudreygraham
www.bregraham.com

Senior Acquisitions Editor	Stephanie Milner
Editorial Director	Cara Armstrong
Design Manager	Marianne Markham
Project Editor	Lucy Sienkowska
Senior Designer	Tania Gomes
US Editor	Jennette ElNaggar
Senior Production Editor	Tony Phipps
Senior Production Controller	Stephanie McConnell
Jacket and Sales Material Coordinator	Jasmin Lennie
Art Director	Maxine Pedliham
Publishing Director	Katie Cowan
Editorial	Nicola Graimes, Sarah Epton, Angie Hipkin
Design	Evi-O. Studio	Kait Polkinghorne
Photography	Issy Croker
Food and Prop Styling	Emily Ezekiel

First American Edition, 2023
Published in the United States by DK Publishing,
a division of Penguin Random House LLC
1745 Broadway, 20th Floor, New York, NY 10019

A catalog record for this book
is available from the Library of Congress.
ISBN 978-0-7440-6959-4

DK books are available at special discounts when purchased
in bulk for sales promotions, premiums, fund-raising,
or educational use. For details, contact:
DK Publishing Special Markets,
1745 Broadway, 20th Floor, New York, NY 10019
SpecialSales@dk.com

Printed and bound in China

www.dk.com